The flooers
am the

for

FRIENDS IN SANDY BELL'S
PAST AND PRESENT

HAMISH HENDERSON

A Critical Appreciation

Ian Spring

First published 2020
by Rymour Books
45 Needless Road
PERTH
EH1 2JU

ISBN 978-1-8381863-3-3

Cover design by Ian Spring
Printed and bound by
Imprint Digital
Seychelles Farm
Upton Pyne
Exeter

The paper used in this book is approved
by the Forest Stewardship Council

CONTENTS

ACKNOWLEDGEMENTS

Jim Black and Fred Freeman have read versions of this essay and I thank them for their input and their friendship. Kätzel Henderson gave me permission to quote in full the poems and songs of Hamish Henderson in the appendices to the book.

The front cover features a fascinating portrait of Henderson by Charles Naysmyth and I am grateful for the artist's permission to reproduce it. For other illustrations I would like to thank Michael McVeigh, Joy Hendry and Dave Cossar. The portrait featured on internal flyleaves is based on a photograph by the late Sharon Bunt.

Ruby McCann and Calum Smith helped at the final stages with the editing and proofreading.

Over the years I've had many stimulating conversations with friends of myself and Hamish Henderson in Sandy Bell's, aka The Forresthill Bar. This book is for them.

FOREWORD

This volume is an expanded version of the essay that served as the centrepiece for a volume of essays on topics inspired by Hamish Henderson—*Hamush Henderson and Scottish Folk Song* (2015). That essay was titled 'Hamish Henderson: Man and Myth' and that title has proved prescient in the last few years as the mythology of Henderson has proliferated. All mythologies deserve to be interrogated and this volume begins and ends with a consideration of the myth of Hamish Henderson.

The original essay was written rather quickly. I stated (rather boastfully as it sounds now) that it had taken me seven days to write as opposed to the seven years it took for Tim Neat to write his biography. The point I was trying to make rather crassly was that an instantaneous and hopefully coherent account from a personal point of view was the objective of that piece. This work has taken longer and is more considered and, hopefully, objective. In the original essay, I referred to the subject as 'Hamish'. In this revision I refer to him as 'Henderson', more in keeping with an academic essay. However, there is one area in which my objectivity may be challenged: there are several occasions on which my analysis of the work of Hamish Henderson relies on my own personal experience and recall of conversations with him. Therefore, I have been unable to erase my own person from the book, even for the sake of critical distance. So I still refer to myself in the first person.

The title of this volume is *Hamish Henderson: a critical appreciation* which I think fairly reflects the nature of the piece. I considered titling it *Hamish Henderson: a critical introduction.* I hope it will serve as an introduction and encourage new work based on Hamish's life and ideas but I think the title as decided is most accurate.

Also, this essay is not simply an academic survey of Henderson's work. It is also a polemic and expresses my own viewpoint (briefly) on a range of issues. Since I criticise, directly or tangentially, those who have indulged in anecdote and unwarranted speculation regarding Henderson, it is unfortunate that I cannot write from a more distant and impartial viewpoint. However, that cannot be. Critical work on Henderson by scholars more distant from the man himself is welcome. The only substantive piece of this nature recently published is Corey Gibson's excellent *The Voice of the People: Hamish Henderson and Scottish Cultural Politics* and I refer to this throughout this book.

Fred Freeman kindly wrote a preface to *Hamish Henderson and Scottish Folk Song* and noted:

> What Ian Spring has grasped, in endeavouring to debunk much of the Hamish Henderson myth, is a more complex idea of the man—and, indeed, a more comprehensive idea of human culture. He sees clearly that there is a vertical and a horizontal dimension to the man, Henderson, and to art in general, be it folk song or what have you. Without that vertical and horizontal, we are all like the frogs at the bottom of the well looking at a circular piece of sky. Consider, for a moment, Hamish's bold appeal for a cultural revolution throughout Britain and Ireland: ' ...the time has come for contemporary art-poets to renew their energies – not in debate in university seminar rooms, not in the pages of small magazines, but in direct contact with the folk poets. Intellectual enquiry is one thing, art something else.'
>
> Art poets and folk poets carrying-out precisely that 'fruitful cross-fertilisation' that he discerns in the whole corpus of 'the Scottish cultural tradition' over the previous thousand years or more.

In many respects Spring's own approach owes a great deal to this school of thought; pays tribute to the ideas and the man behind them.

Hopefully, this book addresses the multi-dimensional aspects of Henderson's work and his legacy and stresses the complexity of the issues arising from his work. This complexity, I feel, has largely been elided by the tide of adulatory prose that has recently arisen.

In relation to this, I refer to two assumptions about Hamish Henderson's career as 'myths': firstly that he devoted his entire time to the folk tradition rather than his own writing; secondly, that he wished his own poetry to be preserved purely by oral transmission (rather than in printed form). To be absolutely clear, I am suggesting that these assumptions may be partially true, but are not *absolutely* correct, and need to be reexamined by any serious critic.

Hamish Henderson was such a powerful and charismatic figure that it is not surprising that a wealth of anecdote and speculation has arisen around his memory. The mythology surrounding Hamish has partly been perpetuated by the two-volume biography penned by Timothy Neat. This is a massive and important work of scholarship and erudition, but it is tainted by unwarranted and sometimes bizarre speculation that stretches the reader's credulity.

More recently much has been written and spoken about Henderson. An annual festival, the Carrying Stream Festival, run by the Edinburgh Folk Club, has a Hamish Henderson lecture (annual lectures have also been organised by Colin Fox, of the Scottish Socialist Party). The texts of some of these have been published. The tone of them I would generally describe as uncritical and anecdotal. At this crucial juncture in the history of the Scotland, I would suggest, any reassessment of Hamish

Henderson's contribution to twentieth-century Scottish cultural history will have to move beyond anecdote and speculation and engage with the issues of culture, art and nationhood emerging in this new century.

So, what is the extent and importance of that contribution. To those who have embraced him enthusiastically, he is a tower of strength in modern Scottish literature. However, in the published scholarly summaries of Scottish literature he gets scant mention. Hopefully, this will change as more scholars come to terms with his work. With regard to his poems and songs, the collection edited some time by Raymond Ross has been recently superceded by the extended collection edited by Corey Gibson which includes additional poems unearthed, largely, by Timothy Neat from the archive collection of Henderson's papers. This reveals a greater depth and compass to his poetic work and encourages further study.

The mythologising, the 'beatification', of Hamish Henderson has been a process that I, at least partly, have subscribed to, and I have been aware for some time that it should be addressed. What I have tried to do in this essay, to the best of my ability, is present a realistic portrayal, from both my personal knowledge and from a study of his works, of the nature of Henderson's legacy, of his achievements and his failures, his virtues and his shortcomings.

If the result is to nudge him a little from his pedestal, I believe that it is a sacrifice that Henderson himself would willingly have made to ensure a continuing and egalitarian Scottish cultural community. It is a clichéd phrase, but Henderson epitomised it completely. He was a true man of the people. The legacy of Hamish Henderson will reside in those, like myself, who he helped and inspired. For the future, however, it has to develop in those who approach his published work and collections anew, and those who will have a hand in the future development of Scottish culture, the folksong movement and the political destiny of the Scottish nation.

LIFE

HAMISH

I suppose this essay, although it will mostly be read by those who knew Hamish Henderson or at least have heard of his reputation, should begin with an introduction to the man. My intention is to try to say something about his place in Scottish culture after a period of reflection following his death in 2002, but, to begin with, here is an obituary – one of two I wrote for Henderson, this one shortly after his death for an online journal.

> The death of Hamish Henderson, noted Scottish poet and folklorist and 'the father of the Scottish folk revival', in March this year, sparked a spontaneous show of national grief, with hundreds packing St Mary's Episcopal Cathedral in Edinburgh for the funeral, tributes posted in every corner of the national media, and poems and songs recited in his honour across Scotland and further afield.
>
> Hamish's appeal was both national and international. He loved Scotland and championed its culture and arts, but he opposed Fascism (he had encountered Hitler in thirties Germany), fought with the Italian partisans when serving as an army intelligence officer (he personally accepted the surrender of the Italian troops from Field Marshal Graziani), championed the cause of Nelson Mandela long before it was common or fashionable to do so, and was the first to translate Gramsci into English. His award-winning war-time collection of poems, *Elegies for the Dead in Cyrenaica*, remains a classic of the genre.
>
> Hamish was also committed to interdisciplinarity and,

in his fifty-odd years as an academic at the University of Edinburgh, did more than seemed humanly possible to bring scholars from every discipline and every corner of the world together. I well remember some years ago, when the University had finally agreed to allow an honours degree to be offered by the School of Scottish Studies, Hamish railed against the pedantic decision of the Faculty to name it a degree in 'Scottish Ethnology', rather than simply Scottish Studies or Scottish Folklore. (He also once refused to write a piece for the *Journal of Peasant Studies* because he didn't think the traditional singers he was working with would like to be called 'peasants').

Numerous obituaries have lauded Hamish's qualities as a poet, a scholar and a political activist. However, in the 28 years that I knew him, what struck me most was his irreverence, unfailing good humour and refusal to accept any hidebound orthodoxy. His favourite folksong collector was not Gavin Greig or Francis James Child but the persevering Peter Buchan, a northerner often snubbed by Scott or Kirkpatrick Sharpe and almost bankrupted by his peers. Despite Buchan's sometimes sycophantic Toryism, Hamish had a great regard for his common touch and, when singing or reciting a bit of bawdry would often state that 'Auld Peter', who collected the ribald *Secret Songs of Silence,* would love it.

He championed the work of Buchan and also his namesake, the late David Buchan, whilst still demonstrating that the latter's excellent work *The Ballad and the Folk* was based on a substantial misconception. While Spike Milligan and others lampooned William McGonagall, Hamish wrote an article claiming his place in a northern Irish tradition of popular poetry. His curiosity knew no bounds and he once researched a folksong found as a few words scratched on a shard of pottery. He planned, but never completed, a series of documentaries on individual songs similar to the *Song Histories* of Robert Ford, another under-valued collector.

A quixotic period in Hamish's life was during the eighties when his constant companion was a mongrel dog named Sandy (named after Sandy Bell, the eponymous erstwhile proprietor of Hamish's favourite bar). Hamish was tremendously fond of Sandy who was an incorrigible rogue, effectively debarring Hamish from his local Italian restaurant. Sandy would try to escape from the crack in Sandy Bell's to the nearby Meadows *à la recherche de l'amour*, and Hamish would then inveigle myself or another companion to try to hunt him down!

Hamish was irredeemably untidy. He used to keep a bundle of precious old broadsheets and chapbooks in a pile beside used newspapers in his kitchen, but in his office in what was, effectively, the attic of the School of Scottish Studies, he would shuffle the piles of papers and reveal some stunning manuscript or book or letters from around the world. An unlikely mix of visitors would often meet there and the conversation could range from the films of Fritz Lang through Rabelais to the poems of C P Cavafy. Songs would be sung in Scots, Italian or Gaelic, etc, according to those in attendance.

A healthy lust for life always typified his attitude. Once, during the Edinburgh Festival, when, if memory serves me, he actually slipped on a banana skin and broke his leg, I visited him in hospital to find him far from despondent,

> regaling his visitors with story and song. However, Hamish also had a great respect for death, exemplified in his fine poem 'The Flyting o' Life and Daith'. In 1980, I met him in the Green Hotel, Kinross when the death of his great collaborator in another 'flyting', Hugh MacDiarmid, was announced. The last time I saw him, some weeks before his death, I brought him news of the death of the Glasgow poet, Freddy Anderson and, despite his infirmity, I could sense him striving to recall some whimsical memories of Freddy.
>
> Once Hamish told me that he imagined that when it was his time to go, the bells would ring out over Auld Reekie and his friends would drink a dram to him at the bar in Sandy Bell's. A great many Tomatins and Glenmorangies were toppled throughout Edinburgh this March in memory of this inspirational man.

Two things strike me on reading this in retrospect. One is that some of it might not be true! Because of my defective memory and also, perhaps, because Henderson was not slow, sometimes, to exercise a little poetic licence in his telling of things in the cause of a good story. The second is that it is a little romantic and sentimental, especially in its last paragraph. However, it *is* an obituary – but one of the things I want to address is why much of what is written and said about Henderson today still remains stuck in a rather maudlin discourse. Immediately after Henderson's death many of us hoped he wouldn't be forgotten, that his work would be the subject of a scholarly discourse and would promulgate a continued interest in the areas of Scottish cultural history he promoted. Well, that has not exactly happened. What has happened is that a great deal has been written (and said) about Henderson since his death. However, most of this cannot be called scholarly or academic, or objective or even impartial. Why is this? Well, it is least partly due to what I can only call a cult of adulation that has grown around Henderson which has resulted in the mythologising of his life. I intend to address that issue first.

Hamish Henderson, according to the dust-jacket blurb for Timothy Neat's two-volume biography: ' …lived one of the great lives of twentieth-century Scotland, a dramatic life of epic European scale, a life of major artistic, political and spiritual achievement.'[1] To what extent is this true? Well, it is certainly true that, like many other men of letters, his involvement with the Second World War and the historical and ideological discourses that arose during the mid-twentieth century, were crucial in determining his writing and creative life. Also, he lived a life in which he had to grapple with two contrasting trends: the macrocosmic impulse of high Modernism and the grand narratives and the microcosm of the Scottish people's tradition which he unearthed, preserved and showcased. This led to some interesting dilemmas in his creative and cultural life. Regarding his 'achievement' there is an important issue, as it has been said often enough that Henderson's life was one of unfulfilled promise; that he could have, but didn't, leave the legacy of written work that his talents should have ensured. Of course, this assumption can be reviewed with hindsight in light of the considerable amount of unpublished work that has been unearthed more recently. However, it is certainly true to say that the body of Henderson's work lacks any substantial monograph subsequent to the release of his *Elegies for the Dead in Cyrenaica*.[2] The fragmentary nature of his published work thereafter does create problems for any scholar trying to come to terms with his legacy. Also, the wealth of anecdotal evidence, much of it apocryphal, tends to obscure the nature of his political and cultural vision. Gibson addresses this point in the introduction to his book.

> The idea of Henderson as a focal point where various strands of cultural and political life meet is complemented by the notion that his 'conviviality' was in fact an important part of his armoury, consciously deployed to promote his cultural-political agenda. Though this aspect is impossible to measure, it sits alongside his written corpus, and is very near the surface in any panegyric on Henderson. In one sense, this legacy will be short-lived if it relies on personal reminiscences and kind-hearted sketches of a tall, ambling, slightly shabby intellectual, gregarious, opinionated, always ready to burst into song, holding court in the unofficial headquarters of the Scottish folk revival, Sandy Bell's Pub in Edinburgh's Old Town. In another sense, Henderson cannot simply be cast as a folk hero whose value is in his absorption of a variety of political and cultural concerns. The purpose of this book is to consider what Henderson's legacy might be if it is to be drawn solely from his writings.[3]

Another contrast in Henderson's life is based on an enigma this has not been explained, at least to my satisfaction: that is, how could Henderson, the illegitimate son of a housekeeper brought up in a cottage in rural Perthshire, go on to public school and Cambridge.[4] There is no easy answer to this, but one thing is quite clear – on returning from the War,

Henderson had two choices, based roughly on these unreconcilable elements to his life, and he made a crucial decision – which was not to seek his future career amongst the Leavisites of Oxbridge, but instead to look for it among the rural folk of Scotland and Ireland. The reconciliation of the two strands of his life, I think, was always at the back of his mind. The rest of this study will consider, in tandem, to what extent did he succeed in that quest and, to what extent has the critical appreciation of Hamish Henderson's career and work developed since his death.

References:

1.Timothy Neat, *Hamish Henderson: a Biography, Volume 1: The Making of the Poet (1919-1953)* (Edinburgh: Polygon, 2007).

2. Hamish Henderson, *Elegies for the Dead in Cyrenaica* (London: John Lehmann, 1948).

3. Corey Wilson, *The Voice of the People: Hamish Henderson and Scottish Cultural Politics* (Edinburgh: Edinburgh University Press, 2015), p. 5. The central section is itself part of a mythology.

4. The mystery of his parentage is supposedly solved in Timothy Neat's biography, but there is still speculation – most notably around the Duke of Atholl.

FOUR PICTURES

Where do we search for the spirit of Hamish Henderson today? Well, as good a place as any to start would be in his second home, an office away from the office, Sandy Bell's on Forrest Road. Amongst several images of Henderson therein (the most notable being a papier mache bust that sits above the gantry accompanied by a bottle of malt) there is, framed centrally above the fireplace, a print of a painting by the Edinburgh artist, Charles Naysmith, of Hamish Henderson.

> ...Richard Demarco, who has been making meaningful and often controversial conversation about art for decades, suggested I paint a portrait of Hamish Henderson. I was intrigued by the challenge. Hamish as a poet, a writer, a polemicist and brilliant Cambridge-educated linguist, was very much a man of words and a lot more besides, Even as a soldier and intelligence officer, able to interrogate captured German and Italian officers, his main weapon was words and his lifelong engagement with Scotland's folk music could not be separated from the narrative of song. The journey Richard Demarco had sent me on would be to re-explore the vital but problematic relationship between the world of words and the silent art of painting.[1]

Naysmith did not personally know Hamish Henderson but met with his wife, Kätzel, to research the project. The substance of the painting, therefore, bears the fruits of this research but also seems to construct into an iconic whole many of the aspects of a mythology that has arisen around Henderson.

Henderson sits in his office in front of a desk loaded with papers (untidy, but not as untidy as his actual office, as those who knew him will attest) his dog Sandy sits at his feet and a framed photograph of his wife Kätzel is on the desk – dating the image and giving it a personal context. Henderson's face looks into the distance in a serious and thoughtful manner and is mirrored by a similar profile of himself as a younger army officer on the mantelpiece. Images on a pinboard on the wall reflect his Scottish folk and literary interests through Jeannie Robertson and William McGonagall, but the international context of his work is evident in the portraits of Nelson Mandela and Antonio Gramsci. Similarly reflecting the folk and literary, or Scottish and international context, of Henderson's work, an effigy of a Green Man is built into the mantelpiece and a model of the Lion of Judah (a symbol of Judaism but also, perhaps, of the desert) sits on his desk.

In this timeless image are accumulated, it seems, all the strands of Henderson's life and work, with Henderson in the centre, resting and still gazing, perhaps, towards the future.

Two other paintings featuring also follow this pattern of Henderson surrounded by his influences and friends. Sandy Moffat's 'Scotland's Voices' (featured on the cover of the 100th anniversary edition of the *Collected Poems*) seems to be in a hilly pastoral setting. In the background, an ethereal couple dance exuberantly in the company of a symbolical white horse. In the foreground, surrounding Henderson, who is recording on a reel-to-reel tape recorder, are several figures of the Scottish folk revival: Willie Scott (with his sheepdog), Jean Redpath, Aly Bain, Belle Stewart, Jimmy MacBeath, Dolina MacLennan, Allan MacDonald and Jeannie Robertson. Also featured in the background, however, are the less likely trio of Hugh MacDiarmid, Antonio Gramsci and Heinrich Heine.

Michael McVeigh's painting of The Edinburgh People's Festival Ceilidh, which took place in the Oddfellow's Hall, opposite Sandy Bell's, in 1951, again features Henderson in the centre addressing a crowd of drinkers and chatterers. A couple are winching in the background, a piper is playing, a man, apparently, praying and there is another horse (a frequent visitor to McVeigh's work).[2]

The strange thing is that these pictures, retrospectively produced after Henderson's death, all portray him as at that 'centre' of things. This is in contrast to his experience of being at the *periphery* of things; part of a counter-culture that was never accepted by the establishment of the time. His relationship with the University of Edinburgh was never an easy one, he was largely ignored by the media, especially the BBC, and he was regarded generally as only a minor figure in the Scottish literary revival, with no extensive body of published work and never fully accepted into the Milne's Bar coterie dominated by MacDiarmid, .

Hindsight, however, has treated Henderson and his reputation perhaps more kindly than the Scottish literary and critical establishment ever did.

The legend of Hamish Henderson has taken a while to accumulate its, by now, loaded mythology.[3] Timothy Neat's biography, of course, was not published until seven years after his death. However by 2019 and the hundredth anniversary of his birth the Henderson cult was rampant.

By this time, there were two annual festivals in his honour: The Carrying Stream Festival in Edinburgh and the Hamish

Matters Festival in Blairgowrie. BBC Alba had produced a documentary on his work, *A' toirt suil beatha Sheumais MhicEanraig*. During the year there were several concerts, readings, two plays about Henderson, and a book of poems in his honour was launched at the Edinburgh International Book Festival.[4] The Scottish parliament debated a motion in his honour (containing the completely fictitous suggestion that he 'helped smuggle Jews to safety from Nazi Germany')[5] and, among the slightly more bizarre events, the artist Martin McGuinness created an earthwork portrait of Henderson on a Perthshire hillside. It consisted of reels of black dyed jute held to the earth with steel pine (it took four weeks to constuct and lasted four weeks). Also, the Perthshire poet Jim Mackintosh proposed that 'Hamish Henderson's 1954 meeting with Alex and Belle Stewart in the Cleves field by the Standing Stones on the Essendy Road near Blairgowrie was one of the finest ever examples of a 'Literary Salon' where creative minds met to share songs and stories, to ensure the old wasn't forgotten but to encourage and inspire the new.'

Accompanied this extravaganza of celebration and adulation, however, there was also a great deal of misinformation abroad which prompted me to circulate this short piece:

> Regarding some of the things you may have heard or read: Hamish was probably not 'the greatest Scotsman of (the twentieth) or any other century' (lecture in Edinburgh) or 'a father of Scotland' (*The Courier*) whatever that means! 'The Freedom-Come-All-Ye' was not 'sung on the battlefields of World War Two' (it was written in 1960). Hamish was not the founder of the Edinburgh People's Festival or the School of

Scottish Studies. Hamish was not one of the 'great thinkers' of the century promoting Gramsci's Marxist theory (he didn't care much about theory or philosophy). Hamish didn't punch Alan Bold in Milne's Bar in the cause of the Scottish cultural renaissance and he was not the subject of an assassination attempt by the South African secret police. Having a dram with Hamish in Sandy Bell's (as I often did) was an enjoyable experience but I doubt if it was 'like sharing a whisky with Jackson Pollock in lower Manhattan, or lucking out with a gimlet (with) Graham Greene' *(The Courier*).

One good example of how hyperbole has created a false mythology is in regard to the Edinburgh People's Festival. Henderson did not create this Festival. The Edinburgh People's Festival was founded by the Edinburgh Labour Festival Committee led by Martin Milligan. It does not take any researcher long to discover this as Henderson wrote about it himself.[6] Henderson's task was to organise the concomitant ceilidh (an important event in itself). However, the popular belief, against all evidence, is that Henderson founded the Festival. And of course, the People's Festival was, arguably, the progenitor of the Edinburgh Festival Fringe. So Downing College, Cambridge, on their website, celebrate Henderson as 'Hamish Henderson: father of the 'Fringe''. Such misinformation is rife and is repeated, I have discovered, almost every time Hamish Henderson crops up in a conversation.

Around about this time a good article by the poet Hugh McMillan on Hamish Henderson appeared in *The Herald.* However, it had a strange title (chosen by the paper's sub, not by the author: ' …Scotland's neglected poet'. 'Neglected'?

Tim Neat's detailed, if quixotic, 672-page biography plus Alec Finlay's excellent edition of his letters make Henderson's life just about the most examined of any Scottish man of letters of the twentieth century! Yet, this title is part of a mythology itself and interestingly reflects on Henderson's career (continuing several years after his death) when his work *was* neglected. And I will argue through much of the rest of this study, he has been neglected in the sense that, in parallel with the gathering popularity and notability of Hamish Henderson the person, there has, in general, been a decline in critical work on the areas he promoted and valued: the folk tradition, Scottish cultural history and political identity. The only notable exception to this trend has been Corey Gibson's interesting *The Voice of the People: Hamish Henderson and Scottish Cultural Politics.*[7]

It is concerning that what is almost a cult of personality can serve to obfuscate ideas and debate. And where is the forum to develop some of his ideas? In a time of political strife and mass popular movements, where is the cultural engagement with key questions of personal and national Identity? Where are the *Stone Voices*, *The Eclipse of Scottish Culture*, *Scotch Reels*? Where should we look in now for the multidisciplinary debate on the issues engendered by Henderson's life and work?

Henderson was not a saint, he was not a hero. He was a man of great generosity and tremendous heart who was an inspiration to a whole generation of poets, singers and scholars including myself. So it is time to stop repeating the same old shibboleths and get on with the task of promoting Scottish tradition and culture as Henderson would have wanted us to. Fortunately, there are signs that a new generation are directing their attention to Henderson and are beginning to engage with quite complex ideas in an innovative way. Hopefully, this study will give a little direction to their efforts by picking through some of the morass of misinformation and aiming towards a critical assessment of Hamish Henderson's work.

References:

1. Notes provided by Charles Naysmith.

2. Astute readers will note that the chapter title refers to *four* pictures. The fourth, which goes unheralded, is a montage not dissimilar in effect to the others mentioned that I produced when reframing all the pictures and ephemera as part of the refurbishment of Sandy Bell's in 2013, and it can still be referred to there.

3. In the interim period a bronze bust of Henderson was erected at the Gyle in Edinburgh, and his words sculpted into the area of The Writers Museum and the Scottish Parliament.

4. Jim Mackintosh (ed.) *The Darg* (Stonehaven: The Poet's Republic, 2019).

5. Motion S5M-16000: Joan McAlpine, South Scotland, Scottish National Party: 'That the Parliament notes that 2019 marks the centenary of the birth of Hamish Henderson, who it considers was one of the most brilliant Scots of his age; acknowledges that he was a poet, scholar, songwriter, folklorist, a co-founder of the University of Edinburgh's School of Scottish Studies and the catalyst of Scotland's post-war folk revival; notes that Hamish was born to a single mother in Blairgowrie on 11 November 1919, and went on to win a scholarship to study modern languages at Cambridge; understands that he helped smuggle Jews to safety from Nazi Germany while a visiting student in the 1930s; praises his distinguished service as an intelligence officer in the Second World War, when he oversaw the

drafting of the Italian surrender order of Marshal Graziani; notes that Hamish translated the prison diaries of Antonio Gramsci; praises his poetry collection, *Elegies For The Dead in Cyrenaica*, which received the Somerset Maugham Award; notes that, after the war, Hamish taught with the Workers Educational Association, founded the Edinburgh People's Festival and began collecting and recording folksongs and stories from across the country, including South Scotland, which form part of the 9,000 field recordings at the School of Scottish Studies, where Hamish taught from 1951 to 1987; understands that he brought bearers of Scotland's oral tradition, including travelling people such as Belle Stewart and Jeannie Robertson, to international attention; considers that Hamish wrote many beloved folksongs, including 'Freedom Come All Ye', 'John MacLean March' and 'The 51st Highland Division's Farewell to Sicily'; remembers Hamish as an internationalist who campaigned for Scottish home rule, an end to apartheid in South Africa and nuclear disarmament; notes that he died in 2002 and is survived by his widow, Kätzel, and his daughters, Janet and Christine; understands that events are planned to mark his centenary, including in November at the Hamish Matters Festival in Blairgowrie and the Carrying Stream Festival at Edinburgh Folk Club, as well as in publications such as *The Darg,* a new anthology in tribute to Hamish by The Poets Republic Press; anticipates more events commemorating Hamish's legacy throughout 2019, and believes that these are a fitting tribute to what it considers a visionary talent whose contribution to Scottish culture remains immense.

Supported by: Stuart McMillan, Alex Neil, Neil Findlay, Bill Kidd, Richard Lyle, Kenneth Gibson, Stewart Stevenson, Gillian Martin, Sandra White, Ruth Maguire, Annabelle Ewing, Jenny Gilruth, David Torrance, Fulton MacGregor, Ross Greer, Clare Adamson, Angela Constance, Maureen Watt, Tom Arthur, Claire Baker, Gil Paterson, Gail Ross, Emma Harper, John Mason

Current Status: Achieved Cross Party Support

6. Eberhard Bort (ed.) *'Tis [sic] Sixty Years Since: The 1951 Edinburgh People's Festival and the Scottish Folk Revival* (Ochtertyre: Gracenote Publications, 2011).

7. Corey Wilson, *The Voice of the People: Hamish Henderson and Scottish Cultural Politics* (Edinburgh: Edinburgh University Press, 2015).

AN EXAMINED LIFE

Hamish Henderson was such a powerful and charismatic figure that it is not surprising that a wealth of anecdote and speculation has arisen around his memory. However, the mythology surrounding Henderson has largely been perpetuated by the two-volume biography penned by Timothy Neat. This is a massive and important work of scholarship and erudition, but it is tainted by unwarranted and sometimes bizarre speculation that stretches the reader's credulity. My view is that any re-assessment of Hamish Henderson's contribution to twentieth-century Scottish cultural history will have to move beyond anecdote and speculation. Therefore, I wish, initially, to address some of the mythologies that have arisen regarding Henderson's life and work.

After Henderson's death, some of my fellow scholars thought that a short published account of his life and achievement (somewhat like the Fontana series of short paperback lives of authors) would be welcome. That didn't happen. Timothy Neat obtained a Scottish Arts Council grant, and determined to write a massive two-volume biography (eventually weighing in at nearly 800 pages). It would be seven years before it was complete.

Neat's belief was that Henderson had a 'biographical impulse'. He explains this in his Preface:

> Despite [Hamish's] huge gifts as an art-poet, he spent the best years of his life encouraging others to be 'makars' and his nation to 'sing again'… Why did Hamish not write an autobiography? Why did he discourage the various

> biographers who made offers? Hamish knew he had a life-story well worth the telling. He started a personal archive at the age of eight! By the time he retired from the School of Scottish Studies in 1987 this had become a treasure-house of 'everything concerning people', and included a huge correspondence with a worldwide network of friends and colleagues on a vast range of subjects. He also knew that a great deal of 'disinformation' about his life and work had been circulated and that a 'biographical account' was the obvious means of setting the crooked road straight. During the 1980s he did write a series of semi-autobiographical essays for the Scottish literary magazine *Cencrastus,* and in the nineties collaborated with Alec Finlay on the publication of two books, *Alias MacAlias* (a selection of essays) and *The Armstrong Nose* (a collection of letters). But, with regard to his life as a whole, Hamish consciously and deliberately remained silent. The reasons for this silence were both personal and ideological – and they made the writing of this biography a doubly challenging responsibility.[2]

Neat then decides to detail just about every aspect of Henderson's life, including the mundane: you can read in the biography about Henderson paying his electricity bill, loaning someone £10 that he couldn't afford, being swindled out of money in his latter years by a friend. Was this what Henderson wanted? Part of his 'biographical impulse'? On consideration, I have become to doubt it. Why should this man who dedicated a great deal of his time helping others, acting as a catalyst to others' work; who, arguably, eschewed writing in deference to the oral tradition and spoke little about his own background in public want his life to be recorded in this way.

The result of Neat's biography is that Hamish Henderson now has one of the most 'examined' lives of the twentieth century: more so than most of the other Scottish writers of his time, or indeed any time.

But Neat has a purpose, and that is to take the most mundane and quotidian aspects of Henderson's life and to build them into a grander scheme of things – a plan, that Henderson apparently had from the age of eight when he started his 'archive', a concept that Neat is fond of (but more of that later). Thus, on returning from the War, when Henderson breaks ties with a friend (or maybe sweetheart), he does so because 'he now knew his sacred duty to be: service of the Scottish people.'[3] Could this be the case, or could the concept of Henderson dedicating his life at the age of twenty-five to saving Scotland be just a romantic delusion.

Timothy Neat regards Henderson's role post-war (when he was still unemployed) as so important that he is determined to discover a plot against him. He comes up with a bizarre speculation – that MI5 got him a job at Edinburgh University! '[Helen Cruikshank] may have been alerting Henderson to the fact that MI5 was maintaining an interest in his activities. If this was so, a question arises, was Henderson's appointment to the School of Scottish Studies also influenced by the interests or the demands of MI5… The University of Edinburgh has had a long relationship with the British Intelligence Services and it seems improbable that Henderson would have been given a university appointment without 'a nod' of approval from MI5. If such a nod was given… The inference must be that 'field folk collecting' was seen as a means of diverting and controlling Henderson's revolutionary energies.'[4] Does it not stretch credulity to believe that the British secret service were so interested in folksong scholarship?

Another myth that has been perpetuated regarding Henderson is that the South African secret service intended to 'assassinate' him. I merely ask, if they wanted to, why didn't they?

Another example of this unwarranted exaggeration of Henderson's intentions at the time when, like many, he had returned from the War, still a young man, and was trying to find a way in life, regards a period during which Henderson was on his uppers and had no fixed abode:

> So on he wandered – as he was to do for ten years – seeking poets and finding shelter wherever a sympathetic ear, pocket or friend would house him. Indeed, it was not until Henderson married, in 1959, that he got himself a genuinely permanent place of abode. Not surprisingly, Henderson's need of a bed was to become infamous! So much so that the obsolete Scots word 'to sorn' was reintroduced into the language. 'To sorn: to come for supper and lodge for a month' is how the writer Alastair Reid has defined it, or 'to do a Henderson' as one of the less charitable muttered… Henderson's wandering lifestyle was partly a product of need, but also a consciously didactic act: he wanted to nurture 'charity' in his fellow man, and he wanted to test the 'human will' in Scotland.

I remember, but I can't find a reference, that someone wrote an online review of the biography that didn't remain online for long. It suggested in blunt terms that the contemporary term for 'sorning' was 'sponging'. However, Neat switches the necessity of hard times round to the intentional act of 'testing people's kindness'. Similarly, Neat believed, regarding Henderson's mongrel dog Sandy, that he brought to the pub, that Henderson had deliberately chosen an irascible, badly-trained dog to test people's love of animals!

Henderson could sometimes be belligerent, and it is commonly known that he got into fights with two other poets – Alan Bold and Norman MacCaig. One well recorded incident took place in Milne's Bar. Neat tells the story thus:

> ...I saw Hamish wander forward to where Alan Bold was draped over the bar. Hamish showed his teeth and a great forced smile spread over his face. The teeth were false, they had been made especially for the BBC documentary *The Dead, the Innocent*, and he hadn't worn them for years! He leaned forward, close-up to Alan and said: 'I put my teeth in Alan Bold!' Alan leaned back, have ring and conciliatory. Hamish said again: 'I put my teeth in Alan Bold!' Then he drew himself up to his full height and said, 'I do not like you Alan Bold!' He set his jaw, closed his right fist and very slowly - in slow-motion – delivered an upper-cut that gently grazed Bold's chin. He repeated the gesture, announcing loudly – 'I do not like you Alan Bold!' It was a challenge to fight and the barmen quickly moved in. Hamish was escorted out, without protest. It was a memorable moment.'[5]

I was not present at that particular incident (although I know someone who was and who has told me an alternative story) but this account is surely unduly dramatic. In any case, why elevate a drunken squabble into some sort of heroic poetic stance. We should remind ourselves: punching people is wrong.[6] More importantly, however, it is an attempt to elevate Hamish Henderson to a heroic figure that typifies much of the biography from the very beginning.[7] Corey Gibson notes that 'Henderson's holistic approach to academic and creative work, making no distinction between poetry and song, and engaging directly in the 'folk process' while seeking to understand it, has perhaps encouraged his admirers to adopt a similar approach. As a result, a body of text like the 'Flytings' is homogenised into this rendering of Henderson as 'folk-hero', battling for his political vision and its foundation in the radical folk tradition.'[8] Interestingly, fictionally, Henderson also appears as a heroic figure in a novel by the songwriter Stuart Macgregor. *The Myrtle and the Ivy*.[9] It is puzzling why this heroic mythology, seemingly at odds with the persona of a mild-mannered university academic, seems to have stuck to Henderson. Perhaps it is a throwback to his wartime persona, and yet his wartime poetry is notably humane and anti-heroic.

The points I make above may be seen to be nit-picking, pedantic or inappropriate in the face of the overwhelming desire to romanticise Henderson's contribution to Scottish culture in the twentieth century. However, I do not see it that way. Timothy Neat himself notes that some 'friends' saw it fit to poke fun at the (sometimes) rather shambolic figure of Henderson. I want Hamish Henderson to be taken seriously and his work impartially assessed. Some of these mythologies serve to create a smokescreen that makes this more difficult. Not so long ago a senior academic who knew Henderson only by reputation, said to me something along the lines of 'so it isn't true that Hamish Henderson won the battle of El Alemein and collected all the folksongs in Scotland single-handedly?'

An excessive degree of fancy and hyperbole gets in the way of a proper assessment of Henderson's contribution to Scottish cultural life. It also engenders mythologies that inhibit a critical evaluation that would continue the critical themes that he engendered.

In its detail, its often fascination anecdotes, Its contextualisation of the literary scene in Scotland and Europe, its introduction to the general public of unpublished texts by Henderson, Timothy Neat's biography is one of the great Scottish literary biographies of the last two centuries. However, *pace* the points raised above, it is not a critical biography. There is little evaluation of the impact of his work, its critical reception or the place it occupies in literary and folklore studies.

References

2. Timothy Neat, *Hamish Henderson: a Biography, Volume 1: The Making of the Poet (1919-1953)* (Edinburgh: Polygon, 2007), p. xv.

3. Timothy Neat, *Hamish Henderson: a Biography, Volume 1: The Making of the Poet (1919-1953)* (Edinburgh: Polygon, 2007), p. 175.

4. Timothy Neat, *Hamish Henderson: a Biography, Volume 1: The Making of the Poet (1919-1953)* (Edinburgh: Polygon, 2007), p. 8. Later he adds, 'if MI5 did decide, in 1951, to snuff out Hamish's revolutionary ardour by exhausting him in the impossible task of harvesting 'the Scots folk tradition,' it failed miserably.' Timothy Neat, *Hamish Henderson: a Biography, Volume 1: The Making of the Poet (1919-1953)* (Edinburgh: Polygon, 2007), p. 42. A few years ago, I wrote to the Vice Chancellor of the University of Edinburgh quoting Neat and enquiring if the

University had any explanation for this claim. I received no reply. Neat also states that 'MI5 sought to destabilise the John MacLean Society.' (p. 109).

5. Timothy Neat, *Hamish Henderson: a Biography, Volume 2: Poetry Becomes People (1952-2002)* (Edinburgh: Polygon, 2007), pp 184-185.

6. Henderson apparently also had an antipathy to McCaig which as reputed to have come to blows and an incident is also recalled by Neat, Timothy Neat, *Hamish Henderson: a Biography, Volume 1: The Making of the Poet (1919-1953)* (Edinburgh: Polygon, 2007), p. 211. There were certainly many differences between them. McCaig was a pacifist and a conscientious objector during the War in contrast to Henderson's strong support for military action (against Fascism). Also, McCaig was seen to have sided with Hugh MacDiarmid in the 'flytings' and appeared on McDiarmid's side on a recorded clash regarding the folk tradition which was never broadcast. It was also suggested that McCaig was homophobic.

8. Corey Gibson, *The Voice of the People: Hamish Henderson and Scottish Cultural Politics* (Edinburgh: Edinburgh University Press, 2015), p. 22.

9. Stuart Macgregor. *The Myrtle and the Ivy* (Edinburgh: Macdonald, 1967).

Timothy Neat's biography of Henderson is a strange mixture of hyperbole and euphemism, or exaggeration and evasion. There is one issue regarding Henderson for which evasion has been the trend for some time.

So, as for the spectre at the feast, the issue of Henderson's sexuality, I will cut to the chase. I knew that Henderson was homosexual shortly after I met him. Everyone knew, his colleagues, his friends in Sandy Bell's (everyone it seems except Timothy Neat, who, seemingly, sustained a relationship with Henderson for twelve years without realising it).

Of the major obituaries for Henderson, two – by his long time friends Angus Calder and Raymond Ross mentioned his sexual proclivity briefly, which I regarded as the honest and correct way to address it. I too wrote (another) obituary for Henderson and, to be honest, I can't recall whether I mentioned the issue or not; I certainly did not regard it as of great importance.

However, by the time of Henderson's funeral, the issue had raised its head. There were rumours that Henderson's family were unhappy at it being mentioned at all, that certain people had been 'excluded' from the funeral formalities because of it.

Whether this was true or not, by the time of the delayed publication of Timothy Neat's first volume of Henderson's biography, it *was* addressed as, in actual fact, Henderson's own notebooks detailed an affair with a seventeen-year-old French prostitute in Paris in 1937. Timothy Neat, therefore, feels obliged to deal with it: 'His occasional homosexual 'outbursts' were invariably short, sharp and shocking, to himself as much as to others. However, he refused to be ashamed by what 'life' sometimes delivered and, in both youth and age, he gloried in life's unscripted pleasures.' Strangely, Neat tries to 'justify' Henderson's sexual behaviour on aesthetic and ideological grounds: 'Henderson's fearless sexual amorality was part poetic licence and part revolutionary stance'[1] The odd use of quotation marks and the rather prosaic language, not to mention the strange use of 'outbursts', as if sexual behaviour was a kind of disease, demonstrate Neat's reluctance to deal with the issue and, although he does cover Henderson's attitude to homosexuality later in his biography, he does not mention Henderson's own experiences again directly in the remaining pages of his mammoth work.

So, how do we deal with this issue? Poets, writers, artists (folklorists?) are not noted for their sexual propriety or, indeed, for sober and sensible behaviour in general! Brendan Behan had numerous homosexual encounters that arose, arguably, from his experiences in borstal, Dylan Thomas was notably drunken and promiscuous. The much admired Scottish poet Edwin Morgan was homosexual and the recent biography *The Last Dragon*,[2] discusses his sexual history in detail, including liaisons in Glasgow's public lavatories. With regard to these others, their sexual orientation, their behaviour or indiscretion, has not detracted one whit from their reputation or renown. Indeed, Edwin Morgan was Scotland's 'Makar' and has been lauded as 'Scotland's best-loved poet since Robert Burns.'[3] Why, then, should Neat, or anyone else, act as an apologist for Henderson's not uncommon sexual proclivity? Well, Henderson's sexuality is not important in any reassessment of his work: or is it?

Actually, I think it is. Unlike Morgan, who dealt directly with his sexual experiences in his poetry, Henderson's reference to sex and sexuality are oblique. However, they are important to some of his later poetry especially. Henderson was always interested in bawdry and sexual folksong and he employs, to an extent, Rabelaisian or Bacchanalian scenes of wanton sexuality in his poems as a counterpoint to the sexual repression of the Kirk. An example is in *Auld Reekie's Roses*:

Through Jessie's wanton window
A single bulb still burns
The tall chain-smoking chimney
Stands by while Jessie earns…

The brothel-bank's for bursting,
The inmates all set free.
The Kirk, that four dissembler,
We'll break it's back in three.

Or in these verses from *Floret Silva Undique*:

The bonniest pair ye iver seen
Play chasie on the Meedies green.
Undressed to the nines, frae tit tae toe,
The Kimmers o' Coogate are a' on show.
Ripper o' flies, lord o' the tools,
Yon mental boot boy Eros rules…

Whae's yon chattin' up Jess Mackay?
It's Bailie Burke, wi' his weet wall-eye.
The kinchin's bara, so clinch the deal:
gie her a note, son, and hae a feel.

Edina—Reekie—mon amour.
Dae't, or I'll skelp your airse, ye hoor.
The flesh is bruckle, the fiend is slee:
Susanna's elders are on the spree.
The bailie beareth the belle away.
The lily, the rose, the rose I lay…

Whit dae ye hear amang the broom?
Spreid your thies, lass, and gie me room.
Twa gaed tae the woods, and three cam hame
Reekie, tell me my true love's name.
Edinburgh castle, toun and tour
The gowans gay and the gillieflοor.
Luvers daffin' aneath the slae
Floret silva undique
The bonniest pair ye iver seen
Fuckin' aneath the flooer'in' gean.
Baimies wankin' abuin the clay…

The obvious comparison is with Sydney Goodsir Smith:

Flat on her back seven nichts o the week,
Earnan her breid wi her hurdies' see it.

The haill toun at it,
Aa the lichts pip-poppan
In and out and in again
I' the bits and bend
And single ends,
The banks and braes

O' the toueran cliffs o lands…
Given owner entire
Til the joukerie-poukerie![4]

Henderson did appreciate Goodsir Smith. Neat suggests that they were good friends and that Henderson valued his judgement.[5] However, I do know (he told me) that Henderson had reservations about some of Smith's work, regarding it as over-literary and complex compared to his more direct style (he especially thought that Goodsir Smith's *Carotid Cornucopious,* a sort of Joycean Scots stream of consciousness novel, was too abstruse). With this in mind, there are distinct differences in the two approaches: Smith's style is more artificial and sometimes surreal. Henderson uses colloquialisms and folk speech (as he did throughout his career) and the style is more direct. I believe that, in the later Edinburgh poems, Henderson was close to finding a style that would merge the two major influences on his poetry, and I will address that later in this study.

In essence, ribaldry and bawdry occur throughout Henderson's poetic work and they find their expression from his war-time days and the parodies and sexual folk songs through to the later Edinburgh poems. As Raymond Ross points out, 'the strong satiric vein which runs throughout the poetry is not unconnected with celebration of *libido*… the poet is of the devil's party.'[6] The bawdy was commonplace to Henderson, not something on the fringes of folk culture or poetry. Fred Freeman notes, 'the bawdy is, in certain respects, Henderson's ultimate folk voice.'[7]

Largely due to the hegemony of the Kirk in Victorian Scotland the elements of bawdry popularized by Burns and others in the late eighteenth and early nineteenth centuries were expurged: 'this was an era when many Scots were devoting themselves to empire building, and the numerous songbooks that we are produced became repositories of the 'refined', the mawkishly sentimental and the braggaficio-patriotic… ' However, here is little doubt that the substance of the bawdy strain in the folk tradition was freely available to Henderson. Burns's *Merry Muses of Caledonia* was available in several editions, one, notable, edited by Sydney Goodsir Smith and James Barke.[9]

However, a parallel collection, Peter Buchan's *Secret Songs of Silence*, was of particular interest to Henderson. This collection, which Buchan attempted but failed to publish during his lifetime, had been bought for Harvard University Library by Francis James Child (with the assistance of the Scottish bibliophile, William MacMath) and had languished in the archives there for half a century before Henderson became aware of it.

In the 1950s, Henderson was in correspondence with Gershon Legman, a folklorist and collector of erotica who had worked with Alfred Kinsey, the sexologist. Also, in 1954, Henderson had come across the American folklorist, Ken Goldstein, who eventually, despite some opposition, obtained a Fulbright Scholarship to visit Scotland in 1959 and worked with Henderson on the 'Scots Tinker Project'. On 7th September 1959, Gershon Legman wrote to Henderson, 'Ken Goldstein, who as you know was editing folksong records for a company in New York, has got a scholarship to spend a year in Edinburgh. I asked him to try to have made and take along for you a copy of the Buchan 'Songs of Silence' MS, of which I understand there is no copy in Scotland.' On 16th October, Legman further wrote: 'Glad to hear Goldstein is on his way to carry the torch of ethnology to darkest Buchan… I have told him of the 90 MS volumes of Gavin Greig's ballad collections (the Shame of Scotland that they have never been published, my worthies!)… By the way, was he able to get the photoprint copy of Peter Buchan's 'Secret Songs of Silence' to bring to you? (I sent special permission to Univ. Microfilms)… '[10]

In fact, the *Secret Songs* manuscript was, we might say (aping Legman's ascertation that the manuscript had been 'smuggled' out of Scotland by MacMath on behalf of Child) 'smuggled' back home to Scotland and Henderson had great pleasure in showing it to a variety of scholars, including Alexander Keith. Henderson's desire was to disseminate the songs in the manuscript as widely as possible and that is how, some years later, a copy came my possession and it was eventually published in its entirety. Another major scholar to take an interest in the *Secret Songs* was Bert (A L) Lloyd, author of the seminal work *Folksong in England*, who actually sang some of the songs. In this manner, during the early days of the folksong revival in England, led by Lloyd and Ewan MacColl, some of the songs were passed onto, and recorded by, younger performers – for example, *The Bedmaking* and *The Devil and the Feathery Wife* by Martin Carthy and *The Whirlie Whorl* by Anne Briggs.

In a way, Henderson's interest is rescuing the bowlerised from exile was, and he saw it as, a microcosm of the process of recerding and disseminating the folk tradition in general. As he states:

> The trouble here in Scotland has been, and still is, that the elite are to a big extent also the elect, and consequently have a vested interest in keeping songs of the damned well battened

down under hatches. Firmly entrenched in all positions of administration, religion and the organisation of culture, the elect deny just as long as they are able that anything so vulgar as popular culture exists… For folk-song is an elusive thing, and captivity is hateful to it. Those who wish to coat it with rouge and greasepaint find inevitably that they must first turn it into a cadaver. The history of Scottish folksong-ism has been chiefly a determined attempt to take all the guts and spunk, all the ardour. verve and raucle randiness out of the song of the people, and reduce it to the level of a kirk social.[11]

Another avenue out of Calvinistic repression that Henderson investigated was the secret society of The Horseman's Word.

Henderson's other great anthropological 'discovery' was the secret society of the Horseman's Word. Henderson saw the Horseman's Word as an organisation of the damned calvinist dogma divided society into the elect and the damned and, echoing his writings on folksongand the elect of the elite who conspired to suppress or else sanitize it. Henderson describes the secret society as part of the struggle of folk culture to gain hold in a society that cannot sanction such modes of collective self-expression without delegitimatising it's own establishment. The distinction between the ploughman and the travellers is quite clear: the former seek out clandestine organisations in an effort to practice a folk culture of their own, where has the latter are free from any need to resist as they live… [12]

I first became aware of the Horseman's Word, the ancient secret of Scottish ploughmen, also known as the Society of the Horseman's Word, when, sometime around 1974, Hamish Henderson gave me an offprint of an article he had written on it for the *Scots Magazine*.[13] This is how he describes the initiation ceremony and it is worth quoting in full as it not only a good description of the rite but a piece of descriptive writing of some merit:

> The number of initiates taking part in the caper had to be an odd number, preferably thirteen; the place chosen was always a barn a good bit off the beaten track. To avoid detection, the locale of meeting was changed frequently. When the seniors of the cult had collected the names of sufficient novices, they passed around the word to attend; this was sometimes done by sending a single horsehair in an envelope to the brother invited.
>
> Each novice was told of the summons to attend by a 'made Horseman.' He was also told that he had to bring with him a bottle of whisky, a jar of berries (or jam), and a loaf of bread. There is a verse of *Nicky Tams*, often sung and seldom understood, which puts the matter succinctly:
>
> It's first I gaed on for baillie loon,
> An' syne I gaed on for third:
> An' syne of course I had to get
> The Horseman's grip an' Word.[2]
>
> On the appointed night, when the rest of the farm world were safely bedded, the novices were roused and convoyed

across country to the barn selected for the ceremony. On the way they were blindfolded. When the horsemen got to the door of the barn, they gave the 'horseman's knock'(three measured raps), pawed three times on the door with hands or feet, and whinnied like horses. Inside the door stood the 'minister,' and the following interrogation took place –

'Who cometh? In the name of the Word speak your name.'
'A brother.'
'A Brother of what?'
'Of horsemanry,'
'Who bade you come here?'
'The Devil'
'What way did ye come? The crooked way, or the straight way of the path?'
'By the hooks and crooks of the road.'
'In what light did ye come ?'
'The stars and the light of the moon.'
'What's the tender of the oath?'
'Hele, conceal, never reveal: neither write, nor dite, nor recite: nor cut, nor carve, nor write in sand.'

Towards midnight the ceremony began. The novices, still blindfolded, knelt in a circle around the 'minister,' each with his left foot bare and his left hand raised. The 'minister' rehearsed the mysteries of the Word: he told the lads the name of the first Horseman, which was Cain… and gave them the Word itself, which was another word written backwards. He also revealed the two verses of the Bible which were to be read backwards when a Horseman wished to invoke the aid of the Devil.

As the novices received the Word they swore 'neither to write, nor dite, nor recite it.' Immediately afterwards the 'minister' tried to trick them into breaking their oath. The blindfold would be raised slightly to allow each boy to see paper in front of him, and the command would be given – 'Now you have the Word: write it.'

Occasionally a sharp lad would be fly enough to refuse, but the average greenhorn fell for the trick. He would take the proffered pen or pencil to write the Word, but before he could write the first letter he would be given a 'lick' over the fingers with the backchain of a cart or the stock of a horsewhip. Several old men to whom I have talked in Buchan and Stra'bogie still bear the marks of this 'lick' on their fingers.

After this – the ritual infliction of pain – the novices were pushed one by one into the cauf-hoose of the barn for 'a shak o' Auld Hornie.' No horseman was a right 'made Horseman' if he had not shaken hands with the Devil, so everyone had to go through it. Sometimes the 'Deil' was a man dressed in a calf-skin rubbed with phosphorus; sometimes he was a live calf or goat. In either case, the novice felt a hoof pressed into his hand, and he was ordered to shake it.

This completed the initiation.

After it the bottles of whisky were uncorked, and the meeting became less formal… As the drinking got going, the horsemen would challenge each other on points of horsemanry and rehearse a number of esoteric shibboleths. One question often put was – 'Where were ye made a Horseman?' To this the correct answer went as follows:

In a Horseman's hall
where the sun never shone
where the wind never blew
where a cock never crew.
and the feet of a maiden
never trod.

Henderson's observations on the Horseman's Word were informed by the many taped conversations he had conducted with source singers and horsemen from the North-East in the 1940s and 50s, notably with the ploughman Jock Ainslie, but it is fictionalised for the purposes of the popular press.

The Society of the Horseman's Word, is essence, drew together several strands of Henderson interest in the folk process: the suppression of bawdry, the underground folk process in opposition to the constraints of Calvinism and the preservation of itinerant groups such as the ploughman and the travelling folk.

However, there are a couple of serious caveats regarding Henderson's 'discovery' of the Horseman's Word. Firstly, he did not discover it. In fact, the society had been 'exposed' as early as 1881 by William Singer[14] in a widely circulated pamphlet. The Glasgow bothy ballad collector, John Ord had also written about it.

The *Scots Magazine* article was not the first written 'expose' that Henderson had made of the Horseman's Word. He had written the following letter to the *Manchester Guardian* in 1954:[15]

The 'Horseman's Word', in its heyday, was a mass

> organization, and the Kirk was powerless to interfere with it. At its initiation ceremonies the blindfolded novices had to 'hae a shak' o' auld Hornie' ('shake of the Devil's hand'). The 'Devil' was usually a calf or a goat, and the novice had to 'shake' its hoof. As late as 1914, a goat was kept year in and year out in an isolated Aberdeenshire bothy, for no other purpose than to take part in the ceremonies of the 'Horseman's Word'.
>
> Sometimes the young lads were badly maltreated at these ceremonies: if they could be tricked into breaking part of the initiation oath, they were beaten with a 'nickie tam' (leather thong), or the back-chain of a cart. Many old men are still alive in the north of Scotland who carry on their bodies marks of this ordeal. The ceremonies of the Horseman's Word ended in what can properly be described as orgies. Toasts were drunk, defying Kirk and State, and exalting the world, the flesh, and the Deil. The newly elected novices each contributed a bottle of whisky, and the horseman staggered out into the early dawn all 'bleezin' drunk'. There is an old man alive today, in a mental hospital in the north of Scotland who, when a boy, was driven out of his wits by the well stage-managed effects at one of these ceremonies. I am reluctant for obvious reasons to mention the names in the case, but I am in possession of the facts.

Yet much of this cannot be substantiated, and it also concentrates on the more sensationalist aspects of the Society and its ceremonies. In fact, it *is* the more sensationalist aspects of the cult that fascinated Henderson. Timothy Neat records a private conversation with him: 'I knew I had entered a Cave of Gold… Going out in the moonlight to those black byres to find men parading in calfskins and blind-folded boys suspended from hooks was mind-blowing. In the lantern-light, the horsemen looked as if they had just ridden in from the steppe. Here was theatre of a high order.[16]

So, it is clearly these dramatic elements of the ceremony that interested Henderson, but there is a more mundane aspect of the Society in that the Horseman's Word served, before the building of the Farm Servants' Union in the North-east, as a bulwark against the exploitation by the farmers. The initiated horsemen were pledged to give the younger members every help that lay in their power. If a lad at the start of his service was inefficient, he could be sure that the older 'horsemen' would tutor him and would pull him through. In a substantial essay on the subject, I conclude that the Horseman's Word was, in fact, more mundane and never so secret, so widespread nor so focused on the diabolical as it has been given credit for.

Yet the 'glamour' of the Horseman's Word and its associated rituals has continued to be popular. *The Horseman's Word* is the title of a novel by Georgess McHargue and by Neil Roy, a BBC television drama from the 1980s and a memoir of country life by Roger Garfitt from 2012. There are various poems that mention the Word including a poem sequence by Edwin Morgan.[17]

In fact, it is interesting that Henderson and Morgan were both interested in the Horseman's Word and there is possibly a tentative link:

> Alec Finlay admired both Hamish Henderson and Edwin Morgan, and tended to see a link between these writers and his father's work, and also with the folksong movement of the 1960s which Henderson did much to encourage. in his

> view, all three formed a nexus against the high modernism of MacDiarmid and his followers, which colour as we have seen, had tended to close down certain avenues of artistic exploration. his reading of the period was that both Henderson and Morgan use the secret cult of the Horseman's Word – an initiation ceremony into the exclusive world of Scottish ploughmen which Henderson had been given entry during his folklore research in the Highlands – as a way to hint at gay subculture.[18]

Corey Gibson also notes that, 'Henderson's description of the this society's whisky-fuelled initiation ceremony, too, was subtly homoerotic, with the young novices being 'tricked into what into breaking part of the initiation oath' so that they would be 'beaten with a 'nickie tam' (leather thong), or the back-chain of a cart.'[19]

Whether woven into the question of homosexuality or not, I think that Henderson's fascination with this subject was part of a wider interest in subversive Dionysian, Bachanalian ceremonies or occasions that are part of a folk tradition in Scotland (compare the ribald 'The Ball of Kirriemuir') but also throughout world folklore. This interest was to resurface in his later poems.

Interestingly, a recent article of Henderson focuses on just this tradition

> For Henderson, the promotion of Scotland's folk tradition, what he referred to as 'The Underground of Folk Song', was synonymous with the (re)discovery of a distinctive pre-Reformation Scottish culture, liberated from both Walter Scott's romanticism and the kitsch of the Kailyard… Based

> upon his own radical reinterpretation of a raw and earthy rural working-class Scottish past, he reimagined Scottish identity as raucous, sexually liberated and whisky-soaked… Mixing sex with drink, Henderson's Dionysian vision of a collective Scottish consciousness was defined by neither one gender nor one sexuality… Henderson's Scottishness was raucous, drunken and very bawdy and, importantly, it challenged the traditional view of Scottishness as a heterosexual masculine construct.[21]

In essence, it was a counter-cultural impulse that drove Henderson's interest in a bawdy Rabelasian tradition For Henderson, bawdry, sexual liberation and licentious celebration continually lurk in the background of Calvin's Scotland and remain themes throughout his life and work.

References:

1. Timothy Neat, *Hamish Henderson: a Biography, Volume 1: The Making of the Poet (1919-1953)* (Edinburgh: Polygon, 2007), pp 28-29.

2. James McGonigal, *The Last Dragon* (Dingwall: Sandstone Press, 2010).

3. James McGonigal, *The Last Dragon* (Dingwall: Sandstone Press, 2010), p. xiii.

4. Sydney Goodsir Smith, *Collected Poems 1941-1975* (London: John Calder, 1975).

5. Timothy Neat, *Hamish Henderson: a Biography, Volume 1: The Making of the Poet (1919-1953)* (Edinburgh: Polygon, 2007), pp 339-40.

6. Raymond Ross, 'Hamish Henderson: in the Midst of Things', *Chapman*, Vol. VIII, No. (Winter, 1985), 11-18, 17.

7. Fred Freeman, 'A New Voice on the Carrying Stream', in Eberhart Bort (ed.) *At hame wi' freedom: essays on Hamish Henderson and the Scottish*

Folk Revival (Ochtertyre: Gracenote, 2012), pp 109-130.

8. Hamish Henderson, *Alias McAlias: Writings on Songs, Folk and Literature*, (Edinburgh: Polygon, 1993), p. 1.

9. Robert Burns, *The Merry Muses of Caledonia*, edited by James Barke and Sydney Goodsir Smith (London: W H Allen & Co, 1965).

10. See Neat, Timothy, *Hamish Henderson: A Biography, Volume 2: Poetry Becomes People* (Edinburgh: Polygon, 2009), p. 7. The details included, which have not been previously published, have been provided by Tim Neat.

11. Henderson, Hamish, 'At the Foot o' Yon Excellin' Brae', in McClure, J Derrick (ed.) *Scotland and the Lowland Tongue* (Aberdeen: Aberdeen University Press, 1983), pp 104-33, p. 120.

12. 19. Corey Gibson, *The Voice of the People: Hamish Henderson and Scottish Cultural Politics* (Edinburgh: Edinburgh University Press, 2015), p. 194.

13. Hamish Henderson, 'The Horseman's Word', *Scots Magazine*, Vol. 87, No. 2 (May, 4. 1967), 2-4. See also Hamish Henderson, 'The Ballad, the Folk and the Oral Tradition', in Edward J Cowan (ed.), *The People's Past* (Edinburgh: Polygon, 1980), pp 97-105 and Hamish Henderson, 'At the Foot o Yon Excellin Brae: The Language of Scots Folksong', in J Derrick McClure *Scotland and the Lowland Tongue* (Aberdeen: Aberdeen University Press, 1983). Henderson also contributed a section on the Horseman's Word to Reader's Digest, *Folklore, Myths and Legends of Britain* (London: Reader's Digest, 1973), pp 462-463 and articles in *Scottish International* and *The New Statesman.* The *Scots Magazine* later published a (very) similar article: Archie McKerracher, 'The Horseman's Word', *Scots Magazine* (January, 1987), 388-393. See also Archie McKerracher, 'The Horseman's Word', *The Countryman* (May-June, 1999), 82-86. Hamish Henderson, *New Statesman* June 1962.

14. William Singer, *An exposition of the Miller and Horseman's Word: or the True System of Raising the Devil* (Aberdeen: James Daniel & Son, 1881).

15. Letter to the *Manchester Guardian*, 20th May 1954. It is followed by examples of 'songs which the horsemen sang at their meetings' which

are, in fact, fairly typical bothy ballads. Printed in Alec Finlay (ed.), *The Armstrong Nose: Selected Letters of Hamish Henderson* (Edinburgh: Polygon, 1996) pp 65-66.

16. Timothy Neat, *Hamish Henderson: a Biography, Volume Two: Poetry Becomes People (1952-2002)* (Edinburgh: Polygon, 2009), p. 5.

17. Edwin Morgan, *The Horseman's Word: a sequence of concrete poems*, (Preston: Akros, 1970).

18. Alec Finlay (ed.), *The Armstrong Nose: Selected Letters of Hamish Henderson* (Edinburgh: Polygon, 1996), p. 334. See also Thomas Gray, 'Turning Their Fey Shoulders to the Wheel', in *The Hamish Henderson Papers*, edited by Steve Byrne (Edinburgh: The Hamish Henderson Archive Trust, 2013), pp 1-13.

19. Corey Gibson, *The Voice of the People: Hamish Henderson and Scottish Cultural Politics* (Edinburgh: Edinburgh University Press, 2015), p. 195.

20. Sarah Leith, 'Sex, Whisky and 'Rock and Reel': Hamish Henderson's Reimagining of Scottish Identity.' online in Scottish Critical Heritage. She adds, making a contemporary connection. 'It must be emphasised that Henderson's reconstructions of both Scottish history and Scottishness are undoubtedly problematic in many respects; for one thing, a Bacchanalian extravaganza of sex, whisky and 'Rock and Reel' is not the everyday reality for people in Scotland, no matter whether they live in a rural Aberdeenshire bothy or in the central belt. However, Henderson's aims to strip Scotland of what he regarded as its nightmarish, repressive tartan plaid and to replace it with something earthier was part of a wider mid-century debate being conducted amongst radical intellectuals and writers to redefine Scottishness and to reconstruct a new and distinctive Scotland. With Scotland in 2019 asserting its distinctiveness within the Union, arguably more than ever before as a result of Brexit, it may now be time to pay attention to Henderson's prophecy that 'Tomorrow, songs/Will flow free again'.

Angus Calder notes that the seminal influence on Henderson's poetry was in fact, Modernism: the later poems of Yeats, of T S Eliot and Ezra Pound. He also notes that: 'the elitism of leading modernists is well documented – not least, that, on occasion, of MacDiarmid.'[1]

After the War, Henderson had returned with pieces of verse which were published in various periodicals, most notably *Penguin New Writing.* Accumulated, these constituted the collection *Elegies for the Dead in Cyrenaica*, published in 1949 as a book, although the poems themselves only extend to 35 pages.

Nevertheless, for a comparatively small collection, The *Elegies* received the exceptional acclaim of being awarded the Somerset Maugham prize that year. The prize had been set up by William Somerset Maugham in 1947 and awarded annually to writers under the age of thirty. A prestigious prize, subsequent winners have included Doris Lessing, Ted Hughes, V S Naipaul, Angela Carter, Douglas Dunn, Julian Barnes, William Boyd and Peter Ackroyd.

However, it is often forgotten that this was not Henderon's first post-war publication. In 1947 a small publication appeared entitled *Ballads of World War II*, supposedly only for members of the fictitious Lili Marlene Club of Glasgow (the name apparently suggested by Hugh MacDiarmid). This volume is best known for the first appearance of three of Hamish's own songs: 'The 51st Highland Division's Farewell to Sicily', 'The Ballad of the D-Day Dodgers' and 'The Ballad of the Taxi Driver's Cap'. The rest is an interesting hash of pieces from the field more or less edited and added to by Henderson. He states in the introduction that he 'refused to insult these ballads by bowdlerising them' and there are variious obscenities as well as some racist content. In common with much of Henderson's later work, the *Ballads* are, in the end, not just his own work but an amalgam of songs, ditties and conversations collected by him. As Gibson notes:

> Henderson drew from a diverse body of source materials in his creative verse: from the folk tradition, the literary canon, classical antiquity, newspapers and popular culture, and perhaps most prominently, from those social spheres he moved through, from the mess halls, battlefields and interrogation rooms of the War, through to the pubs, campfires, kitchens and seminar rooms of his time with the School of Scottish Studies.[2]

Can there be a connection between the *Ballads of World War II* and the substantially more formalised high modernism of the *Elegies*? Well, one thing in common is that the *Elegies* sometimes employ the words of soldiers on the field:

> Morning after. Get moving. Cheerio. Be seeing you
> when this party's over. Right, driver, get weaving.
>
> I wonder how he died? Just as well it was him, though,
> and not one our chaps… Yes, the only good Jerry,
> as they say, is your sort, chum.
> Cheerio, you poor bastard.

As Sorley Maclean states, 'the *Elegies* have their complexities:

juxtapositions of soldiers talk, and sometimes violent but natural outbursts of men much under fire and propaganda, and even the same men in the lulls of warfare and memorable and often noble language'[3]

Secondly, although not at first obvious, the *Elegies* have an orality to a degree. Some individual lines are memorable and, demonstrated by several recordings, much of the *Elegies* can be successfully read aloud. For example:

...Slake
The crushing breakers-hurled rubble of the guns.
Dazzling darkness, we'll wake you! Hell's bells
blind you. Be broken, bleed
deaths head blackness!

Let my words knit what now we lack
The demon and the heritage
And fancy strapped to logic's rock.
A chastened wantonness, a bit
That sets on song a discipline,
A sensuous austerity.

Although an element of the *Elegies,* with its mythological references, quotations in German and Gaelic, etc, courts the obscurity of some modernist literature of the time, there are sections and individual lines which are in themselves striking and memorable.

Of course, the *Elegies* is not merely a collection of poems, but functions as a homogenous whole, reflecting a personal experience and also a more general reflection on a period of history. The actual title is of significance itself. It notably refers not to 'the desert' or any generalized arena of combat but specifically to Cyrenaica, emphasising that the twentieth-century conflict was actually set in part of the ancient world. Cyrenaica (part of Eastern Libya) had been for centuries occupied by both the Greeks and the Romans, and Cyrene itself was an important intellectual centre of the ancient world. As well as a theatre of war, Henderson sees Cyrene as 'a symbol of civilised humanity, of our 'human house'.

According to Gibson, 'The theatre of desert war, then, already belonged to the artistic imagination before the soldiers arrived. It was a site for the collision and detritus of symbols and histories, and Henderson would transpose several landscapes over it, imbuing all with a kind of collective and transcendent memento mori.'[4] Many commentators have pointed out that the desert is a setting of uncertainty, of the mirage, the doppelgänger, embodying uncertainty and endless shifting in form. In essence, the genius of the collection is to reflect the War through the shifting perspectives; the thoughts and suffering of the soldiers amplified through the prism of the desert. Of course, it is also a journey for the poet and a journey of self-discovery that is revealed through the two opposing voices of the verse, the personal, and the more objective and omniscient narrator who takes personal experience and places it in the context of history, legend and mythology. Alex Finlay notes that:

> ...on a personal level the *Elegies* represent his spiritual quest, and this culminates in the day the poet spends wandering amongst the remnants of the Pharaohs' once glorious

empire, searching the Valley of the Kings for Rilke's 'single column'. These real and imaginary fragments of history and culture give a sense of the desert's consuming power. In this desolate, shifting landscape the quest for meaning, the confrontation of an inner spiritual desert of doubt, intensifies his yearning for the shared human values of love and solidarity. The interior emotional struggle begins as a parallel to the exterior political drama, and then merges with it, and finally emerges as the dominant theme.[5]

History, or the nature of history is a continuing theme throughout the *Elegies*. Periods of war, of course, exist almost outside conventional history. The usual recording mechanisms for events become scanty or unavailable and we become more reliant on oral testimony and memory. Famously, of course, the eventual history of wars is written by the victors. In the eighth elegy, 'Karnak', the War becomes 'some war', another repetition in the wider course of history or histories:

> … Observe the king
> as he offers up the spoils of Syria to Osiris.
> No doubt he is acknowledging
> the conclusion of some war to preserve civilisation.

Angus Calder notes that this elegy seems to suggest a cyclical view of history.[6] The War then, becomes one war within wars.

The 'epilogue' to the *Elegies*, 'Heroic Song for the Runners of Cyrene' returns to legend, myth and the ahistoric moment, '…Instant of nothing… down the thunderous cataract of day', in counterpoint to the first elegy of '…No gods and precious few heroes.' It is a retelling of a legend recorded by the Roman scholar Sallust. The cities of Carthage and Cyrene, unable to agree on the boundary between them, agreed that two runners from either city would set off at the same time. Wherever they met the boundary would be set. The runners from Carthage, the Philaeni brothers, progressed further and, to cement their sacrifice for the city, they agreed to be buried alive at the spot. Subsequently, the spot was marked by two pillars, known as the Altars of the Philaeni. In 1937 another monument based on the legend was constructed here by order of Benito Mussolini, the Marble Arch. It was intended as a symbol of the Italian colonisation of Lbya (it was destroyed by order of Colonel Gaddafi in 1973).

The final section of the *Elegies*, therefore, encapulates an ancient and a modern history and can be seen to commemorate individual sacrifice and suffering as a metaphor for conflict.

The 'Heroic Song' is prefaced by a quotation from Denis Saurat: 'Without suffering and death… we should not know the difference between the visions of the intellect and the facts.' The *Elegies* can be viewed as a search for the middle ground between intellect and hard facts subsumed under the continuing impetus of history. And finally, in the 'Heroic Song'

> …History the other
> emerges at last from the heat's trembling mirror

Gibson comments:

> This dialectic is the history of humanity: human civilisation must grapple with the common structures of its past, with

its origins, if it is to be preserved. As Henderson's series culminates with this point, the survivor's guilt that is evoked in earlier verses seems to have been absorbed and superseded by this larger process. Nevertheless, the dialectic is made incarnate through the bodies of the historical runners. The grand narrative of civilisation cannot be extricated from its human cost; the bodies of the contemporary war-dead are, like the runners, physical incarnations of the dialectic.[7]

The *Elegies* are, as a cohesive whole, one of the most powerful expressions of any wartime experience, but they do not constitute the entirety of Henderson's wartime poetry, as Douglas Gifford points out: ' …just before the great elegies the poems change,. As in 'Death as a Dancer' and 'Lines to a Fool': their mood darkens [and] Henderson continued writing powerful war poetry: 'So Long', his laconic farewell to Africa, 'Song for an Irish Red killed in Sicily" and and 'Lament for the Son', where he imagines an Italian father's grief.'[8]

Neat[9] points out, in fact, that Henderson's 'war poetry' can be extended to include a more substantial body of work:

Poems of Germany and the English Home Front (1939-40).
Poems of the Home Front (Scotland) (1939-41).
Songs and Poems of the Pioneers (1940).
Songs of Sabotage and Sedition (1940-45).
Elegies for the Dead in Cyrenaica (1942-47).
Desert Songs from North Africa (1942-43).
Songs and Poems of the Italian Campaign (1943-45).
Poems Translated in a Time of War (1939-46).
Ballads of World War II – in Five Languages (1939-46).

The Bawdy at Home and Abroad (1939-46).
Aphorisms of Heaven and Hell (1939-46).

And yet, returning home after the war, almost fully formed as a poet, Henderson made another choice. Nineteen Forty-Nine was, in effect, the culmination and the end of his career as a Modernist poet. The next decade led him elsewhere. The second section of this study focuses on Henderson's life and work after his return to Scotland.

References:

1. Angus Calder, Introduction to Hamish Henderson, *Alias McAlias: Writings on Songs, Folk and Literature*, (Edinburgh: Polygon, 1993).

2. Corey Gibson, *The Voice of the People: Hamish Henderson and Scottish Cultural Politics* (Edinburgh: Edinburgh University Press, 2015), p. 74.

3. Sorley Maclean, introduction to *Hamish Henderson, Elegies for the Dead in Cyrenaica* (Edinburgh: EUSPB, ND), p.11.

4. Corey Gibson, *The Voice of the People: Hamish Henderson and Scottish Cultural Politics* (Edinburgh: Edinburgh University Press, 2015), p. 49.

5. Alec Finlay (ed.) *The Armstrong Nose: Selected Letters of Hamish Henderson* (Edinburgh: Polygon, 1996), pp 302-303.

6. Angus Calder 'Scottish Poets in the Desert', *Southfields*, 6.1 (1999). Henderson points out that amongst Scottish poets writing about the war in the desert were George Campbell Hay, Sorley MacLean and Robert Garioch. However, they are not widely recorded in the main anthologies published. See 'The Poetry of War in the Middle East, 1939-1945' in Hamish Henderson, *Alias McAlias: Writings on Songs, Folk and Literature*, (Edinburgh: Polygon, 1993), pp 295-297. The

connection between them was indirect, although Alec Finlay notes that the books Henderson claimed to carry throughout the campaign were MacDiarmid's *A Drunk Man Looks at the Thistle*, and the small volumes of poems by Sorley MacLean and Robert Garioch.

7. Corey Gibson, *The Voice of the People: Hamish Henderson and Scottish Cultural Politics* (Edinburgh: Edinburgh University Press, 2015), p. 56.

8. Douglas Gifford, 'Literature and World War II' in Ian Brown & Alan Roach (ed.) *The Edinburgh Companion to Twentieth-Century Scottish Literature* (Edinburgh: Edinburgh University Press, 2009) pp 88-102, pp 94-95.

9. Timothy Neat, *Hamish Henderson: a Biography, Volume One: Poetry Becomes People (1919-1953)* (Edinburgh: Polygon, 2009), p. 351.

WORK

FLYTING

In considering Henderson's work subsequent to the War, firstly, I want to say something about Henderson's relationship with the most famed Scottish poet of the twentieth century, Hugh MacDiarmid. Henderson was familiar with MacDiarmid's work before the War and read his epic *A Drunk Man Looks at the Thistle* whilst in the desert.[1]

They first met on 24th March 1947[2] and they began as friends (MacDiarmid had positively reviewed the *Elegies*) and ended as friends, but in the midst of their careers there occurred two infamous 'flytings', roughly between 1959 and 1964.[2] These consisted of a debate that took place through a sequence of letters to the *Scotsman* newspaper largely on the nature of Scottish poetry and the folk revival. 'Flyting' refers to a formalised form of verbal sparring, originally in verse. MacDiarmid's *cri de couer* in the Scottish Renaissance was 'Back to Dunbar' and possibly the first recorded flyting in Scottish literature was *The Flyting of Dunbar and Kennedie* (1503) although there are other examples in Scottish medieval literature. It is probable that these verbal contests were performed publicly and were mostly vituperative and consisting to a large extent of insults. As regarding the appelation of the letters between Henderson and MacDiarmid, it was Thomas Crawford who originally called them 'flytings'.

These 'flytings' have been discussed in detail in an essay by Raymond Ross,[3] who posits certain oppositions: literary tradition versus folk tradition, hard line Stalinism versus soft soap socialism, etc. However, these oppositions are not as simple as they, at first, seem. Raymond Ross notes: 'The important word, or at least the term I want to focus on from the above 1967 MacDiarmid quotation, is not 'nationalism' which is actually secondary to the (in)famous Henderson-MacDiarmid flyting in late 50s/early 60s in the letters page of the *Scotsman*, but the word 'vision'. If they did both agree that without a vision the people perish, does that mean that they both shared a single 'vision' of things Scottish? The short answer is, of course, an emphatic 'No'. But how far their 'visions' of Scotland, of Scottish culture, of Scotland's future and its place in the world were (in)compatible is a far more vexed and complex question.'

The flyting is seen by some as a crucial intervention in the debate about the value of the folk tradition that led to the folk revival in Scotland. But was this episode in Scottish cultural history as important as some have made it out to be? I think not. For a start, MacDiarmid's political views are sometimes just nonsense and he often adopts positions that are ridiculous just to be thrawn. This is aided by what Ross calls MacDiarmid's 'romantic egotism and psychological solipsism'. It is strange that, in an era when any sort of Scottish cultural renaissance was struggling to find its feet, two advocates of Scottish literature and culture should be in opposition.

The first of the flytings was a bit of a storm in a teacup over the omission of Henderson from an anthology of poetry. Raymond Ross comments: 'The debate, quickly taking on the tones of a full-blown flyting, has already begun about a recently published poetry collection – *Honor'd Shade: An Anthology of New Scottish Poetry to Mark the Bicentenary of the Birth of Robert Burns* (1959) – edited by Norman McCaig, poet and friend of MacDiarmid. The anonymous *Scotsman* reviewer says, among other things, the book 'might perhaps almost' have been called

'The Muse in Rose Street' implying that McCaig's choice of contributors merely reflected the work of the so-called Rose Street group, satellite poets who revolved around planet MacDiarmid, who met and drank regularly together (with or without MacDiarmid) in The Abbotsford and Café Royal: poets and writers like Sydney Goodsir Smith, Tom Scott, Fionn MacColla and McCaig himself.' The debate centred around Henderson's omission from the collection although, apparently, he hadn't submitted anything.

The criticism was that the concentration of work within the volume was centred around a small group or clique of poets who commonly met in Milne's Bar in Rose Street. Also the emphasis was on work in Scots. Suggestions were made regarding how the selection could have been much broader: to include, for example, female poets (there were none), poets writing in English such as Ian Hamilton Finlay, emerging poets, such as the contributors to *Fowrsome Reel*: including Morris Blythman (Thurso Berwick) and Freddy Anderson. This criticism was not acceptable to MacDiarmid whose response was somewhat lofty and arrogant: 'The Rose Street group of contributors are certainly head and shoulders above all the contemporary Scottish versifiers… so far as I am concerned I would like to say that I am satisfied that no contemporary poet deserving inclusion has been excluded.'[4]

Above all, this demonstrates that the Rose Street poets, dominated by MacDiarmid and Norman McCaig, were a sort of cabal dominated by mutual self interest. Henderson was never truly a part of this structure. Whether this was a consequence of his lack of continuing poetic output or whether it precipated the same is a moot point.

The second flyting, known as 'The folksong flyting' was more substantial and involved not just Henderson and MacDiarmid but other figures from the Scottish literary scene such as David Craig and Thomas Crawford.

To grossly simpifly the argument put forward by Henderson and his supporters: the emergence of a great store of folk lierature from the researches of the School of Scottish Studies and others reveals a folk literature that runs parallel to and has equal legitimacy with traditional written literature. Folk performers such as Jeannie Robertson represent it at its height of achievement. Secondly, written literature, including MacDiarmid's, has always, and continues to, draw on folk sources as an inspiration.

The elements of this position are put forward by Henderson:

> [MacDiarmid] goes on making his assertions about the folksong tradition in general, 'What else is Jeannie Robertson doing,' he asks, but promulgating the 'unimproved mass of folksong?' Rhetorical questions are no substitute for argument. An outstanding thing about her versions of songs is precisely their unerring distinction of wording, which is constantly more vivid and poignant than the Child ballad texts; and Ewan MacColl recently collected from an old Perthshire woman's singing a version of 'The Cruel Mother' which ends with a series of metaphors for hell and guilt much more imaginative than the versions known hitherto. Thus the folk tradition improves itself. course, Mr MacDiarmid means improvement by art poets, for whom alone he has any use. Well, Brecht improved folksongs in this sense; so do those great recent works, the radio ballads (eg, the adaptation of

'Windy Old Weather' to describe the slump, in 'Singin' the Fishing')…[5]

Henderson further states his belief in the folksong movement as a future impetus for a genuine national popular culture and also, importantly, as a solution to the perennial problem for Scottish writers, the nature of the Scots language. He also makes an important distinction between language and idiom which will be discussed later in this study:

> …in the long run it is the folksong revival which offers the best hope for a genuine popular poetry, a poetry which, when it gathers strength, will make many of the raucous booths of Tin Pan Alley shut up shop. Our own poets, in particular, will feel a real thrill of liberation when they realize that the primary question facing them is not so much one of language as one of idiom; realize, too, that all resources of a folk-poetry of unrivalled beauty and power are there at their elbow, to help and sustain them – resources hardly comprehended as yet, let alone tapped. Because it sheds light on the language question, and suggests a way out of the Lallans impasse, the folksong revival has much to offer Scots writers. But Mr MacDiarmid sees things differently. Self-criticism can safely be shelved, because the 'summa of the future' will adjust everything. And the widespread interest in folksong which is beginning to affect urban culture all over the world can be written off as 'a fresh wallowing in a mud-bath of ignorance'. Mr MacDiarmid is oblivious of the fact that a revolution is building up all round him.[6]

MacDiarmid's response shows that he certainly seems to be

oblivious, or wishes to be oblivious, to the burgeoning folksong movement, and his attitude to the work the School of Scottish Studies barely stops short of outright contempt:

> Mr Henderson… seems to find his ideal man in the 'muckle sumph', and to wish to scrap all learning and all literature has hitherto to find in favour of the boring toggle of analphabetic and ineducable farm-labourers, tinkers, and the like. He is presumably at home among beatniks and beatchiks. Personally, I continue to think Dante, for example, or Goethe greater poets – and more credible specimens of homo sapiens – than McGonagall are the authors of any – and all – of the 'folksongs' Mr Henderson and his colleagues so assiduously collect. I do not envy the task of whoever may ultimately have to go through the great mass of indiscriminate tape recordings accumulated by the School of Scottish Studies in order to find any elements of real value… such collecting is a waste of time and money.[7]

And subsequently:

> In all literature as there is a vast undergrowth of doggerel and mediocre versifying, (but we shouldn't) believe that this is to be valued as equal to or better than acceptedly great poetry simply because, thanks to their minimal literacy and because it corresponds to their ignorant tastes and reflects the sorry condition of their lives, it is more popular among the broad masses of the people than [examples of high art] …Why should we be concerned then with songs which reflect the educational limitations, the narrow lives, the poor literally

> abilities, of a peasantry we have happily outgrown?… We all know of the great vogue and inter-traffic of European balladry. Most of it is rubbish...and what proportion of the great collection of recordings of the School of Scottish Studies is more than rubbish?[8]

Of course, such offensive statements are part of an exchange of insults rather than any reasoned argument. However, whatever the worth of the folk tradition in terms of its continued preservation, there is no doubt that is has had a constructive influence on Scottish literature and poetry throughout. This is a point made by Thomas Crawford in an intervention in the debate:

> Folksong and some 'high poetry' may be more closely connected than Mr MacDiarmid thinks. Is there not a relationship between the songs in Shakespeare's plays and previously existing folksongs? Were not the lyrics of Goethe's *Faust* influenced by the folksong revival of the late eighteenth century? Does not Blake's imagery owe something to the symbolic traditions of English folksong, which have recently been investigated by members of the English Folk Dance and Song Society? Did not Wordsworth inaugurate a poetic revolution by studying the art and literature of the 'muckle sumphs', and was he not reviled for it in his own day?[9]

In fact, MacDiarmid's own work was influenced by the folk tradition, a fact he does not deny: 'I cannot deny that in Scottish literary history there have been fruitful interactions between folksong and art-poetry, and that this happened in some of my own early lyrics. But… I have had to abandon many of my early ideas and during the last thirty years I have been writing kinds of poetry quite unindebted to any folksong source… '[10]

Here we have a quite gross example of MacDiarmid's own solipsism. The folk tradition was relevant when useful to him and is no longer relevant as he has abandoned it. Of course, the folk and the literary traditions have worked hand in hand in Scotland for centuries, despite MacDiarmid's assertion, and, in retrospect, his often contradictory statements in the flyting seem more a measure of MacDiarmid's own personality than any measure of the debates at the time in the broader area of the developing disciplines of Scottish studies and cultural studies.

Interestingly, it is MacDiarmid's solipsism and his desire to shape Scotland, or his idea of it, within himself, that leads to some of his finest poems. Neat, however, sees this as an essential opposition between Henderson and MacDiarmid: MacDiarmid wishing to shape Scotland and its people to himself, whereas Henderson wishes to shape himself to the people of Scotland.

How important, then, were the flytings within the Scottish Renaissance and general debate on Scottish culture in the 50s and 60s? There is no doubt that they were a rhetorical form of argument (and abuse) rather than any form of logical or considered debate, not helped by MacDiarmid's tendency to take up just about any position that suited his fancy at the time. In fact, MacDiarmid himself did not value the whole episode highly and never mentioned it subsequently. MacDiarmid had many connections within the Scottish scene. How important his connection with Henderson and the flytings was to his subsequent career is debatable, but in Alan Bold's biography of McDiarmid,[11] Henderson is never mentioned, and there are on only two pages very brief mentions of the flytings.

The flytings have been recently revived and have been performed in a stage play, but they largely must be seen as a product of their time. It seems laughable now to consider MacDiarmid's dismissal of the folk tradition and popular culture, but, of course, these flytings come towards the end of the dominance of Leavisite literary criticism and just at the point by which critics such as Richard Hoggart and Raymond Williams were to establish a new critical base from which to regard popular culture and 'the voice of the people'. In fact, Henderson mentions this in one of his letters regarding 'the honour's shade': 'Of late, a new school of Socialist thinking has grown up around *Universities and Left Review*, *The New Reasoner*, Hoggart's *The Uses of Literacy* and Raymond Williams's *Culture and Society*, a school which is not afraid of sociological revaluations, and goes out into the streets to hear not only the 'gamin cry', but the voice and song of the people.' In essence, MacDiarmid's elitist argument was on its way out and, in retrospect, Henderson's position can be seen as prescient in the light of future developments in cultural and literary thinking.

Another way to look at the whole episode of the flytings is as an example of the duplicitous relationship between Henderson and MacDiarmid which can actually be taken further to represent the opposing faces of the Scottish literary revival itself – another form of Caledonian antisyzygy if you like. Gibson notes:

Flyting, and all that comes with it – the performance,

invective, and dialogue – was an appropriate form for Henderson to set out the foundation for his folk revival strategies, and his own work as a poet and song-maker. The collusion that is required in this mode of public dialogue, and the dialectical relationship it represents, are in keeping with Gatherer's image of the two-headed poet. Though Henderson synthesised the work of many figures in his writings, MacDiarmid was his most persistent and resilient influence. In working through his vision of the revival and his conception of the role of literature in society, Henderson found himself embracing MacDiarmid as his dicephalous other.[12]

The relationship between Henderson and MacDiarmid is the subject of one of Henderson's most interesting poems, 'To Hugh MacDiarmid On Reading 'Lucky Poet''. The origin of this poem is particulary intriguing. It is recorded by Gibson and written in 'Merano, September-October, 1945'. According to Neat, Henderson was taking some leave in the Tyrol befor ede-mobilisation: 'In Merano, Hamish completed his reading of Hugh MacDiarmid's chaotic, 'dashed-off' autobiography, *Lucky Poet.* It had arrived in a bundle of books (sent from Heffer's Bookshop in Cambridge, without expectation of payment), while Hamish was on the Anzio Beachhead. Now he read it with concentrated attention and it stimulated a range of powerful responses; within a few hours, he had the bones of a substantial poem, 'To Hugh MacDiarmid, on reading 'Lucky Poet''. Subsequently, apparently, Henderson completed the poem after meeting MacDiarmid two years later but, according to Neat, was advised not to publish it by Louis MacNiece as it would be too controversial to challenge the old man of Scottish letters. It was eventually published in 1967 in a volume to mark MacDiarmid's seventy-fifth birthday. It is suggested by Neat that it could, therefore, be seen as the first exchange in the subsequent flyting with MacDiarmad, but equally, of course, it could be seen as the end of it.

The poem does not read like a early (wartime?) poem of Henderson's. For one thing it employs an unusual form of diction at the end:

> So why all this other junk? Man, I don't get it.
> This problem would soon lay me low – if I let it.
> Amidst all the posturings, tantrums and rages,
> Is there something you haven't said in all these pages?
> Is there some secret room, and you don't want to show it?
> Did an unlucky break befall the Lucky Poet?
>
> Just what do you stand for, MacDiarmid?
> I'm still not certain.
> I don' wanna step behin' dat tartan curtain…

'Man', is a form of direct address not uncommon in North-east Scotland, but, in this context it is perhaps the more contemporary form which suggests the addressee or audience is 'hip' or aware and sympathetic to the speaker. It is also unclear why the particular form of the last line is chosen – as if Henderson's own voice, in the form of direct address to MacDiarmid, has been taken over, almost, by an innocent or scared child.

These are puzzling aspects of what is possibly one of

Henderson's most accomplished poems. There are three elements to the poem. Firstly, it says something about the stance adopted by MacDiarmid:

You admit acting out a superb comedy
Before the Scots burghers, that blubbing company.
Panache weel cockit, sharp sgian in stocking,
But conscious of something (your fighting tail?) lacking,
You strut and you gallivant before them.
Powerless with your piping fancies to fire them
You spurn their blind-alley ways
their shuttered faces
And gar your muse kick high her paces.

You could argue that this sort of positioning is a sort of comment on McDiarmid's entrenched posturing that is typified later in the flytings, but it can also be seen as a wider representation of the powerlessness of the muse against the establishment.

Another opposition that can be teased out is perhaps that of Scotland against England, 'the elephant in the bed':

You tilt against 'Englishism': the words sleek and slick,
The smoothing fingers that add trick to trick;
The admirable refusal to be moved unduly
By the screaming pipe. The desire to speak truly
With a middle voice; the acceptance of protection;
The scorn for enthusiasm, that crude infection…
That's all very well.
But what about 'Scotchiness',

This awful dingy bleary blotchiness?
You list 'Anglophobia' as your recreation,
But it's Scotland that's driven you to ruination!

It is the stifling and repressive ethos of Scottish Calvinism and the sentimentality of the kailyard that Henderson induces as the real enemy of the Scottish psyche:

...The meanness, the rancour,
The philistine baseness, the divisive canker,
The sly Susanna's elder-ism, McGrundyish muck-raking...

...the shame of our idiot Burns Suppers
Which – when poetry's skint, stony broke, on its uppers –
Spend more on a night of befuddled bard-buggering
Than a poet can earn in a year's hugger-muggering,
The couthy Wee McGreegors can still goad you to fury.
You tear coloured strips off their twee tasselled toories...

Here there is more than a reflection on MacDiarmid himself but a sort of treatise for a critique of Scottish culture that this study will interrogate more in its final section.

References:

1. Corey Wilson, *The Voice of the People: Hamish Henderson and Scottish Cultural Politics* (Edinburgh: Edinburgh University Press, 2015), p. 24.
2. Timothy Neat, *Hamish Henderson: a Biography, Volume 1: The Making of the Poet (1919-1953)* (Edinburgh: Polygon, 2007), p. 202.

3. This and subsequent quotes from an unpublished essay by Raymond Ross originally delivered as a lecture at the Scottish National Library.

4. Hamish Henderson, *The Armstrong Nose: Selected Letters of Hamish Henderson*, edited by Alec Finlay (Edinburgh: Polygon, 1996), p. 80.

5. Hamish Henderson, *The Armstrong Nose: Selected Letters of Hamish Henderson*, edited by Alec Finlay (Edinburgh: Polygon, 1996), p. 126.

6. Hamish Henderson, *The Armstrong Nose: Selected Letters of Hamish Henderson*, edited by Alec Finlay (Edinburgh: Polygon, 1996), p. 96.

7. Hamish Henderson, *The Armstrong Nose: Selected Letters of Hamish Henderson*, edited by Alec Finlay (Edinburgh: Polygon, 1996), p. 97.

8. Hamish Henderson, *The Armstrong Nose: Selected Letters of Hamish Henderson*, edited by Alec Finlay (Edinburgh: Polygon, 1996), pp 118-123. MacDiarmid goes on to insult the working people of Scotland! 'Why should we be concerned then with songs which reflect the educational limitations, the narrow lives, the poor literary abilities of a peasantry we have happily outgrown', p. 119.

9. Hamish Henderson, *The Armstrong Nose: Selected Letters of Hamish Henderson*, edited by Alec Finlay (Edinburgh: Polygon, 1996), p. 100.

10. Hamish Henderson, *The Armstrong Nose: Selected Letters of Hamish Henderson*, edited by Alec Finlay (Edinburgh: Polygon, 1996), p. 93.

11. Alan Bold, *MacDiarmid: A Critical Biography* (London:John Murray, 1988).

12. Corey Wilson, *The Voice of the People: Hamish Henderson and Scottish Cultural Politics* (Edinburgh: Edinburgh University Press,

2015), p. 41. Gibson also argues that the form of the flyting has a continuing presence in Scottish cultural debate citing more recent exchanges between Tom Devine and Neil Oliver, and Paul Scott and David Greig. He also suggests that it became a model for self-reflexive debate for the National Collective, a group promoting national autonomy before the first Scottish independence referendum.

MCGONAGALL

Hamish Henderson's production of critical work was comparatively sparse. One reason for this (he told me himself) was that he found the writing of academic prose a slow and arduous process. However, nearly all of his analytical pieces on the folk tradition, poetry, etc (mostly collected under the title *Alias McAlias*) show great critical acumen and insight. The one essay that stuck in my mind on first reading was Henderson's study of McGonagall, *McGonagall the What.*[1] That this was a substantial and serious piece of work is made clear by Timothy Neat: 'It was Hamish who wrote the *Chapbook* article about McGonagall, that it was the longest scholarly article he was ever to write says a great deal about Hamish's ideological 'methodology' and belief in 'the folk process.''[2]

This essay struck me because for the first time it seemed to provide an answer to a perennial bugbear for all students of Scottish literature – the McGonagall Problem. Stated simply, the Problem, concerned with where McGonagall fits into the scheme of Scottish literature, grapples with two opposing theories: 1. McGonagall was a complete fool, tragically unaware of his own limitations and the laughing stock of his more knowing countrymen. 2. McGonagall was not so daft after all, playing to the susceptibilities of his audience, he made a pretty penny.

Of course, neither of these solutions is ideal, nor can they be easily reconciled. However, Henderson's critique of McGonagall, on first reading, seemed to me to offer a middle way. Firstly, and most importantly, Henderson does not accept the accustomed view of McGonagall as unique. Instead, he places his work within the folk tradition:

> Is folk-song ever poetry? Can poetry learn from folk-song? Is there a zone where they overlap, or should we speak rather of co-existence? How and where does money come into the picture? (Or how can we just occasionally keep it out?) These are our themes and our presiding genius is William McGonagall, poet and tragedian, and unchallenged prince of bad verse writers… But – it may be objected – why bring McGonagall into a discussion of folk-song. Surely, when we discuss McGonagall, we are scraping the bucket of uninspired 'art poetry'. What has he got to do with the poetry of the ballads, with the poetry of folksong? Haud your horses – it's not as simple as that. If you have jumped to the conclusion from the title, and these opening paragraphs – that we are going to tie the battered tin-can, McGonagall, to the tail of the folk-song revival, and thus knock its 'image' for good and all, you are quite wrong. However, we have got to face it that a careful scrutiny of the works of McGonagall can teach us a great deal about the nature of folk-poetry… When McGonagall was born, the Coogate of Edinburgh had a big Irish population (still has, in fact); the birthplaces of McGonagall and of James Connolly… are not far apart. Orange and Green are both well represented. The Coogate lies 'contagious' to the Burke-and-Hare axis, which runs in the direction of Surgeon's Hall. McGonagall must have heard, from his cradle onwards and up a rich mixture of Irish and native Scots folklore. In Paisley and Glasgow especially he must have heard umpteen songs with first lines like 'It was upon the twelfth of July in 1690…' Songs with this sort

> of stock opening are still being composed here and there, but in nineteenth-century Scotland and Ireland they were the commonplace of ploughman's bothy and city gin-palace. The drawling 'come-all-ye' tunes brought over to Scotland by bands of Irish labourers must have been very familiar to McGonagall when he was a child, and when he started composing his own poetry.[3]

This way of looking at McGonagall's poetic output, it seems to me, absolves us from the onus of considering McGonagall as a product of the mainstream of the Scottish poetic tradition. Instead, we can consider his work within the context of popular culture and, specifically, of performance (within the context of which McGonagall's work is still immensely popular at suppers, parties, concerts, etc). Once unburdened with the attribution of intentionality and the consideration of McGonagall's individual poetic genius, the opposing conjectures of the McGonagall Problem can, perhaps, be taken as both partially true and, to some extent, reconcilable. McGonagall, in Henderson's model, can be considered not only through the instrument of high literary theory but also from the point of view of genre and generic models of performance and folk tradition.

But, once again, 'haud your horses'! In 'absolving' McGonagall, I have taken one strand of what is a much more complex interaction with McGonagall. In fact, Henderson's interest in McGonagall encompassed both its serious and comic potential, as Timothy Neat points out:

> By the mid fifties Hamish saw McGonagall as 'a leak in the dykeside of half-a-dozen elitist cultural theories!' In 1963

> he helped resurrect the Societas McGonagalliensis at the University of Edinburgh and gave a lecture: 'McGonagall – bard of the poetic belly-flop'. Hamish introduced 'Scotland's most popular poet' with Gramscian seriousness and compared McGonagall's 'long awkward lines' to those used by Dante. He quotes: 'He ran, he put on speed after he had turned away:/ He raced, like the runners on the track at Verona:/ Not like the losers though, but like him who wins the day.' He suggested that McGonagall was a product of folk traditions very similar to those Dante had adapted, and his article triggered worldwide interest… Hamish did not think, or pretend, that McGonagall was a major artist but his bold re-estimation of McGonagall added a dimension to pop aesthetics and literary theory.[5]

With our more pluralistic view of folksong and popular culture today, we have to strain to remember that this period, the 1960s (and through the 1970s) was a period of continuing debate about the nature of 'high' culture and popular culture, with the Leavises aligned against Raymond Williams, Richard Hoggart, etc. It was also a period in which Scottish literature was scarcely valued, even in Scotland. For some time there was only one available text about Scottish literature, written by a German (nowadays there are shelves full). MacDiarmid was so little known that, upon his death in 1979, one national paper proclaimed him as Scotland's greatest Gaelic poet! Nevertheless, there was a burgeoning interest in critical analysis of Scottish culture, evidenced in a variety of small magazines: *Scottish International*, *Cencrastus*, *Calgacus*. The folk revival also agonised over questions of cultural aesthetics: Was folksong art? Was folksong poetry? Was Bob Dylan a folksinger? Was Bob Dylan a poet? These concerns were debated in folk clubs and bars throughout the period. Henderson's evocation of McGonagall, and the questions it raised, therefore, sought to resolve some of these issues. Henderson doesn't leave the question there, however. He also looks for contemporary parallels to McGonagall's work: 'However, although McGonagall is the supreme practitioner of the art of the belly-flop, he turns out to have unexpected rivals. That extraordinary mixed-up genius, Hugh MacDiarmid, has written some of the best poetry Scotland has ever seen, and some of the worst.'[6] This appears as part of the flyting between Henderson and MacDiarmid in the pages of the *Scotsman.* Alec Finlay, in his 'Afterword' to his edited collection of Henderson's letters *The Armstrong Nose*, notes: 'one amusing episode in the skirmish was the use of William McGonagall as a satirical club to beat over MacDiarmid's head'.[7] Henderson gives several examples of McGonagalese from MacDiarmid's poetry including the following:

> Infernal fantasies contrived to hide The simple unacceptable truth!
> — Read Hommel's History of Babylonia,
> And Fink's Die Sprachstamme des Erdkreises, sooth.
> The Atlantis Fable is but a colossal exaggeration
> Of the natural catastrophe of 1031 BC
> Which broke in upon Cornwall – fantastically embellished,
> To hide the simple report of the Scilly Isles tragedy…

Is this form of writing legitimate, or is it merely 'bad' poetry?

Henderson seems to conclusively opt for the latter. Yet is it all that different from the following, from Henderson's own *Glascune and Drumlochy*:[8]

> There were two castles,
> two battled keeps, Drumlochy and Glasclune,
> that kept a bloodfeud bienly on the boil.
> They sat on their airse and they girned fell gyte at ither
> (I'll paisley your fitt', 'I'll brackley your inverey')
> …and atween, the scrogs of the dowdy duddy Lornty.
> Drumlochy's laird was a slew-eye dye-blue bloodhound who fought,
> as his sires had fought, with steel (cold steel!)
> and said the other mugger couldn't take it.
> But Glasclune knew six of that: he was progressive,
> and to be in tune with the times was all his rage.
> Now, one day he went out and bought a cannon
> (a quare old toy unknown to the lad next door):
> with this he gave Drumlochy a thorough pasting —
> dang doon his wall, gave his stately pile the shakes:
> in fact, blockbust him quite.
> 'The moral of this,' said Glasclune, with 'ill-concealed' hidalgo satisfaction, 'is that Right
> — unready starter in the Donnybrook stakes —
> must rise early to possess the field'.

This is based on a legend about feuding families around Blairgowrie, the place of Henderson's birth and was apparently developed in poetry readings in the 1960s.[9] In this 'folk-poem' I believe, we can trace the contrasts that work so well in some of Henderson's work: the *Elegies*, 'The Freedom Come-All-Ye', 'Auld Reekie's Roses'. Colloquialism versus rhetoric, the imagined past versus the immediate present, free verse versus strict metre. However, it has somewhere all gone wrong, any sense of history or immediacy is lost in a confusion of words and images.

Of course, McGonagall represents a folk tradition that runs parallel to the songs collected in the eighteenth and nineteenth centuries.[10] His work was distributed on broadsheets available, for example, in Dundee's Poet's Box, and rubbed shoulders with broadsheets of bothy ballads. It was also a tradition of live performance. He is a central figure in discussions on both the Scottish literary traditions and folk traditions. He features prominently in Charles Naysmith's portrait of Henderson and the artist notes:

> The inclusion of McGonagall's image hovering between the heads of Gramsci and MacDiarmid was no accident. McGonagall's presence in Scotland's cultural story always proves divisive. When working on a book devoted to the hapless bard's life and work, I quickly formed the impression that Scottish evaluations of his significance were highly contradictory; split between ridicule, sentimental affection and a sense of horror that to engage with him at all would undermine the international status of Scotland's culture. Neither Henderson nor MacDiarmid ever suggested that his poetry was anything other than doggerel, but both had felt him worth writing about… For me, McGonagall was a figure who symbolized some of the conflict between 'high art' and 'low art', his very presence in Scotland's cultural

landscape made people think about the issue. He was rather like a great clown impersonating the trials and tribulations of a misunderstood but serious romantic poet. Clowns being first and foremost visual artists, McGonagall lis fascinating not so much for what he wrote but what he acted out. The controversy his name and image arouse seemed to me like a perfect visual metaphor for the conflict between MacDiarmid and Henderson Ultimately, Henderson would probably have preferred a folk tradition without McGonagall, with his fatuous adulation of Queen and empire, and MacDiarmid would have preferred that the folk tradition had not existed at all.[11]

References:

1. Henderson wrote two essays, for *Chapman* and the *New Edinburgh Review*. The longer of these, entitled 'McGonagall the What' is reproduced in Hamish Henderson, *Alias McAlias: Writings on Songs, Folk and Literature* (Edinburgh: Polygon, 1992), pp 274-294.

2. Timothy Neat, *Hamish Henderson: a Biography, Volume 2: Poetry Becomes People (1952-2002)* (Edinburgh: Polygon, 2007), p. 370.

3. Hamish Henderson, *Alias McAlias: Writings on Songs, Folk and Literature* (Edinburgh: Polygon, 1992), pp 275-275.

5. Timothy Neat, *Hamish Henderson: a Biography, Volume 2: Poetry Becomes People (1952-2002)* (Edinburgh: Polygon, 2007), p. 371.

6. Hamish Henderson, *Alias McAlias: Writings on Songs, Folk and Literature* (Edinburgh: Polygon, 1992), p. 289.

7. Alec Finlay (ed.), *The Armstrong Nose: Selected Letters of Hamish Henderson* (Edinburgh: Polygon, 1996), p. 341.

8. Hamish Henderson, *Collected Poems and Songs*, edited by

Raymond Ross (Edinburgh: Curly Snake Publishing, 2000), p. 139. This was described, perhaps surprising, by Henderson as a 'folk-poem' developed through the oral tradition in an essay giving the background. Hamish Henderson, *Alias McAlias: Writings on Songs, Folk and Literature* (Edinburgh: Polygon, 1992), pp 97-100.

9. For more details see Hamish Henderson, *Collected Poems*, edited by Corey Gibson (Edinburgh: Polygon, 2019), pp 24-27.

10. For a discussion on these contrasting aspects of the folk tradition, see Ian Spring, 'Two Collections in the Folk Tradition' in *Hamish Henderson and Scottish Folksong* (Edinburgh: Hog's Back, 2105), pp 262-286.

11. Unpublished notes provided by Charles Naysmith.

Hamish Henderson at the centre of things: Paintings by Michael McVeigh (above) and Charles Naysmith (below)

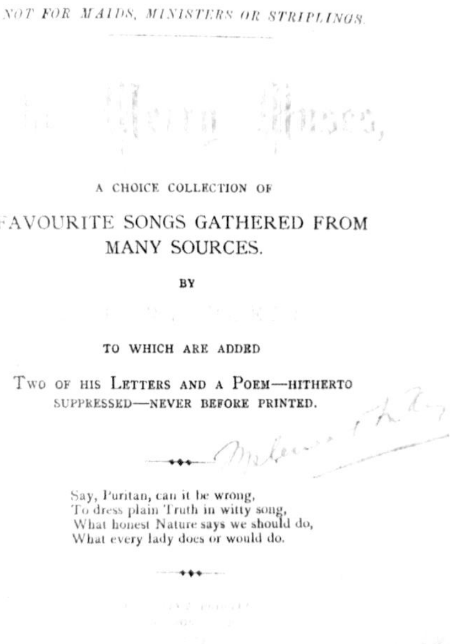
NOT FOR MAIDS, MINISTERS OR STRIPLINGS.

A CHOICE COLLECTION OF

FAVOURITE SONGS GATHERED FROM MANY SOURCES.

BY

TO WHICH ARE ADDED

TWO OF HIS LETTERS AND A POEM—HITHERTO SUPPRESSED—NEVER BEFORE PRINTED.

Say, Puritan, can it be wrong,
To dress plain Truth in witty song,
What honest Nature says we should do,
What every lady does or would do.

Cover page of *The Merry Muses of Caledonian* by Robert Burns. This is one of the spurious '1917' editions actually published in 1903

Peter Buchan, Henderson's favourite ballad collector

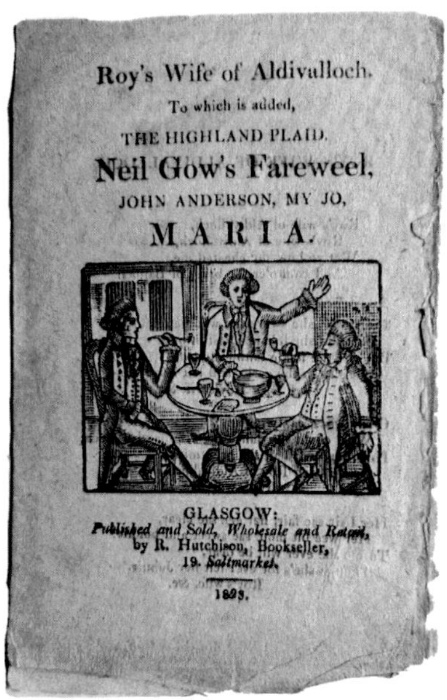
Roy's Wife of Aldivalloch.

To which is added,

THE HIGHLAND PLAID.

Neil Gow's Fareweel,

JOHN ANDERSON, MY JO,

MARIA.

GLASGOW:
Published and Sold, Wholesale and Retail,
by R. Hutchison, Bookseller,
19. Saltmarket.

1823.

A chapbook from Henderson's collection. He understood the relevance of the written word as well as oral tranmission to the folk tradition

William Singer's pamphlet exposing the Horseman's Word (1881)

Cover of *Chapbook* edited by Arthur Argo showing part of the original manuscript for for *The Freedom Come-All-Ye*

Hugh MacDiarmid, Henderson's ofttime sparring partner, as the grand old 'owl' of Scottish letters

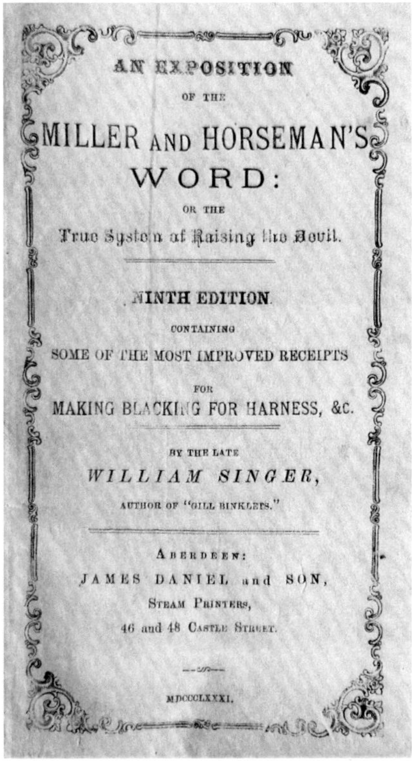

AN EXPOSITION
OF THE
MILLER AND HORSEMAN'S
WORD:
OR THE
True System of Raising the Devil.

NINTH EDITION.
CONTAINING
SOME OF THE MOST IMPROVED RECEIPTS
FOR
MAKING BLACKING FOR HARNESS, &c.

BY THE LATE
WILLIAM SINGER,
AUTHOR OF "GILL BINKLETS."

ABERDEEN:
JAMES DANIEL and SON,
STEAM PRINTERS,
46 and 48 CASTLE STREET.

MDCCCLXXXI.

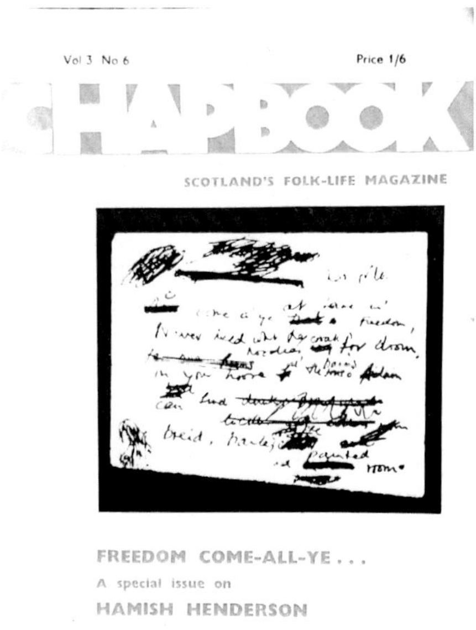

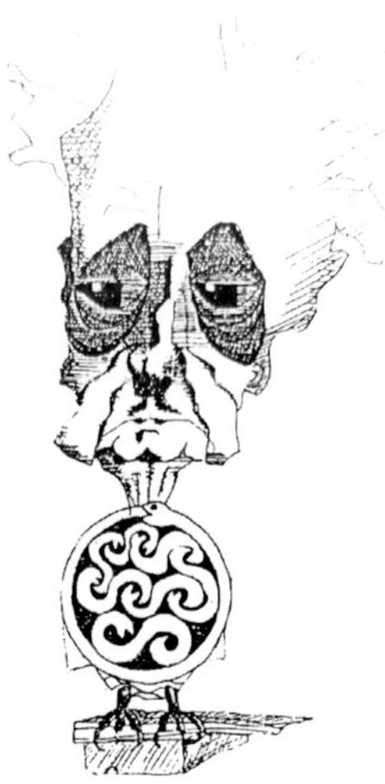

Cover of *Chapman*, edited by Joy Hendry, showing artwork for *The Flyting o' Life and Daith*

Henderson was a prolific letter writer. This letter, to the author, is on the interesting topic of fellatio in Brittany

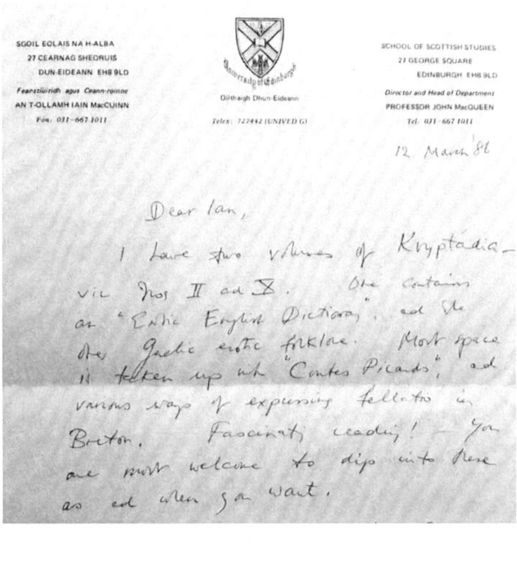

SGOIL EOLAIS NA H-ALBA
27 CEARNAG SHEORUIS
DUN-EIDEANN EH8 9LD
Fear-stiùiridh agus Ceann-roinne
AN T-OLLAMH IAIN MacCUINN
Fòn: 031-667 1011

Oilthaigh Dhun-Eideann
Telex: 727442 (UNIVED G)

SCHOOL OF SCOTTISH STUDIES
27 GEORGE SQUARE
EDINBURGH EH8 9LD
Director and Head of Department
PROFESSOR JOHN MacQUEEN
Tel: 031-667 1011

12 March '86

Dear Ian,

I have two volumes of Kryptadia — viz Nos II and X. One contains an "Erotic English Dictionary", and the other Gaelic erotic folklore. Most space is taken up with "Contes Picards", and various ways of expressing fellatio in Breton. Fascinating reading! — You are most welcome to dip into these as and when you want.

Ewan MacColl (née James Miller), songwriter, playwright and leading light of the Folk Song Revival

Bert (A L) Lloyd, author of *Folk Song in England* (1967)

Cover of *The Rebel's Ceilidh Song Book No 2* (1965)

A contents page for the influential Scottish periodical *Cencrastus* demonstrating a wide range of topics and contributors (1983)

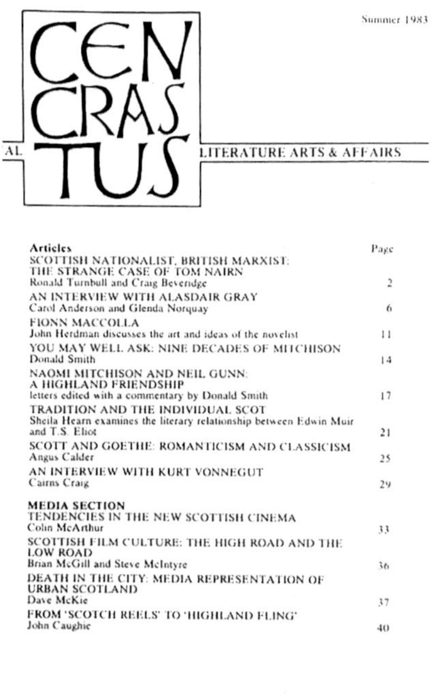
CEN
CRAS
TUS

Summer 1983

AL LITERATURE ARTS & AFFAIRS

Henderson's friend, the Glasgow poet Freddy Anderson

A more recent take on the legacy of John Maclean. Co-opted for the independence referendum of 2014

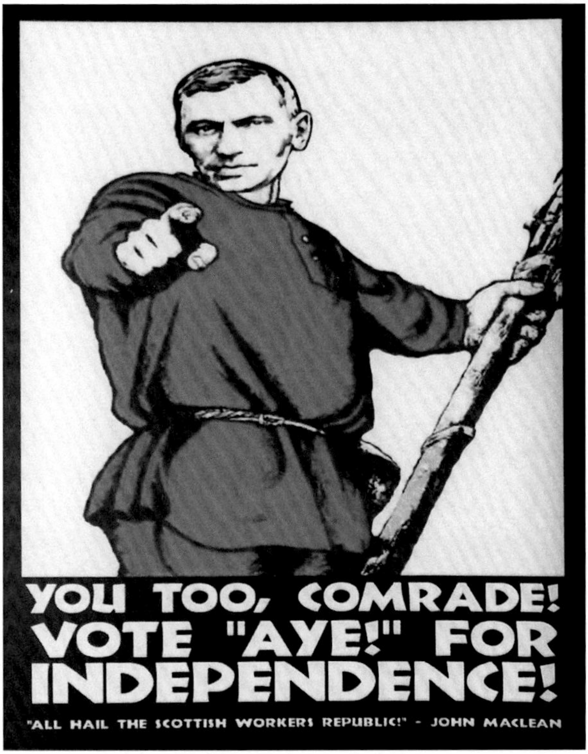

The seminal Heather and Glen LP from the recordings made on Henderson's field trip with Alan Lomax

Cover of *The Darg,* a volume of poems for Hamish Henderson (2019)

Hamish Henderson as many knew him: ordering a drink at the bar at Sandy Bell's

Two observations about Henderson's poetry: firstly, that much of his earlier poetry, such as the *Elegies*, influenced by Eliot and Pound, with its mythological references and its diversity of form, is quite unlike in almost every way, the folk tradition in verse. Secondly, what is especially notable about the body of his poetic work, including the poems and songs, is its linguistic diversity. Henderson quite happily employs German, Latin and Gaelic as well as colloquial Scots, traveller cant and squaddy slang, often combining them in the same work.

To Henderson, I think, 'voice' was all important. His most renowned group of poems, *Elegies for the Dead in Cyrenaica*, stand by themselves and were successful and prize-winning in their time. The key feature of the sequence, however, which fed into Henderson's later work, was the ability to simultaneously combine two voices: the objective and omnipresent voice of the poet; representing history, mythology and the timelessness of life and human conflict and the more immediate, and the, more temporary, voice of the soldier on the ground, experiencing the moment in history.[1]

However, apart from the *Elegies*, what are the key features of the rest of his poems? Well, as stated above, the linguistic diversity, the experimenting with forms (there are a few lyrics reminiscent of MacDiarmid and more metaphysical poems, reminiscent of Edwin Muir) and, undoubtedly, the international flavour of the work. There are versions of, or translations from, a range of European poets: Hölderin (the German romantic features often in Henderson's work)[2], Rilke, Goethe, as well as some less acclaimed figures. One aspect of Henderson's poetic output that has not been seriously considered, in fact, is his work as a translator (and, of course, there is also his important translation of the writings of Gramsci).

Only fairly recently have the key themes in Henderson's poems been examined. Apart from the concern with the authentic voice of the common man, there is, throughout the work, a crucial opposition. Tessa Ransford notes:

> [There are] four strands to guide us in the poetry of Hamish Henderson: firstly his Christian Humanist/Socialism on the pilgrimage journey of his own life, and its demands for commitment; secondly, the journey as one energised by love (eros versus thanatos in an eternal flyting) where beauty overcomes fear even if demanding 'blood and tears'; thirdly Henderson's integrative vision, seeking wholeness in the understanding that the whole is more than the sum of the parts, but that each part is essential to the whole and is related to all other parts, however seemingly fragmented; lastly Henderson's love of company, his sense of the bonds of brotherhood, and his delight in the auditory companionship also of both word and music. Let us call them pilgrimage, love-energy, integration, companionship.[3]

This seems like a good attempt to schematise a complex body of work which will be considered later. Yet it is a fact that, despite his fairly substantial body of work, Henderson's poetry has been largely ignored by literary and cultural critics. Even the *Elegies* have seldom been quoted in war anthologies. Until recently, there was not a single academic article about Henderson's poetry and in the various anthologies of Scottish literature and culture in the twentieth century, there is hardly a mention of Henderson as a writer or poet. It is possible (and it has been done) to moot some sort of establishment conspiracy here. However, my suggestion is perhaps that Henderson's work is too varied and complex to fit neatly into any of the disciplinary paradigms that dictate academic and institutional output today (and in the past). Henderson, perhaps, was labelled as a folklorist and not a poet, and there is no redress to that (Louis Daguerre was a fine painter but he was a primarily known as a photographer so he is not even mentioned in any dictionary of artists!)

However, there is, of course, another explanation. That is that Henderson's poetry was simply not good enough to be critically acclaimed. That is, perhaps, partly true. Yet, there is the feeling that there is, somewhere, a great poem waiting to be written in the latter part of Henderson's life, and that is what I want to consider next.

As we have seen, Henderson's attitude to language is actually quite different to any of his fellow poets. Not only in its use of colloquial spoken English (and that comes through right at the beginning of his career in the *Elegies*) but, especially, in his attitude to Scots in his work. While the Scots literary revival was intent on identifying a pure form of poetic Scots – call it Lallans, Doric, 'plastic' Scots – Henderson instead takes his cue from folk song or 'ballad Scots' and happily employs any mixture of English and Scots that seems to appeal to the ear. He makes this absolutely clear in his essay "At the Foot o' Yon Excellin' Brae': the Language of Scots Folk Song'. Taking Stanley Hyman's contention that Scottish literature was always bilingual, if not multilingual – English, Scots, Gaelic,

Latin – he then identifies a location and practice for writing in Scots/ English: 'If prose and poetry in a self-conscious literary Scots came increasingly to seem documentations of a sad case of arrested development, the anonymous ballad-makers continued on their way, knowing little and caring less of the niceties of hyperborean lingo and prosody. They were, in any case, operating in a zone which ignored national and political boundaries. The themes of the great tragic ballads to which Hyman refers are elemental folk motifs – and many of these cross national language boundaries… This, the idiom in which the virtuoso song-makers were operating, is a flexible formulaic language which grazes ballad-English along the whole of its length, and yet remains clearly identifiable as a distinct folk-literary lingo… Scots may be said to include English and go beyond it.'[4]

Regarding the reservations that some establishment critics may have had about Henderson's poetry, three issues may stand out: his use of the kind of language he mentions above, his use of bawdry and his experimentation with form (notably merging art poetry and song). In his later poetry, I contend, there is a moment when these three fuse together to (almost) produce his finest work.

Henderson, I believe, had thought of the possibility of writing a long sequence about Scotland both prior to and subsequent to the production of the *Elegies*. One dry run might have been 'Journey to a Kingdom', written in the late thirties. Ransford notes, 'It is a stark poem, comparing the conditions of life in the slums of the city to 'early morning by Schiehallion', and the 'lovely tongues' wave-beating language' of the Gaeltachd, where there is still no comfort to be found, since 'Brigades of innocent sheep/ Have put a race to rout.' The poem demonstrates the difficulty of identifying 'community' in Scotland and of reviving it.'[5]

He begins the poem by evoking the slums of Glasgow in a similar fashion to Edwin Muir and Lewis Grassic Gibbon (writing at about the same time):

> Alone and alonie
> I climb Balmano Street. The haggard houses
> Spew out their wizened aged children
> On to the dirty stone…

Then moves on to contrast this with a rather desolate Highlands:

> The ships have sailed
> Past Tomnahurich hill, where men with shoes
> On dry land walked. Brigades of innocent sheep
> Have put a race to rout…

But there is not much more, and, then, I think, the possibility of writing an epic poem about Scotland is forgotten for some decades. When it returns, it is set not in Glasgow or the Highlands of his birth, but in his adopted home, Edinburgh. Henderson was very keen on one poem that he wrote, 'Floret Silva Undique' (I think it was then called 'Auld Reekie's Roses II') and he sent me a copy (in the late 1970s, I think) with a note: '[it is] a variation on the interplay between sex and death *sub specie Calvini*. It takes its refrain, 'Floret Silva Undique' (the woodlands flourish on all sides) from the same treasury of Goliardic song as the *Carmina Burana*… '

The quick and the slaw are game for a tear;
Sma-back snooves from his Greyfriars lair.
Out of the darkmans the queer coves come,
Janus guisers from bield and tomb:
Scrunchit hurdies and raw-bone heid
Junkies mell wi' the livin deid.
Get stuck in Homie, and show's the way.
The lily, the rose, the rose I lay.
Seely sunshine and randy mirk
Like Auld Nick's wing ow'r a pairish Kirk.
Whae's yon chattin' up Jess Mackay?
It's Bailie Burke, wi' his weet wall-eye.
The kinchin's bara, so clinch the deal:
gie her a note, son, and hae a feel.
Edina—Reekie—mon amour.
Dae't, or I'll skelp your airse, ye hoor.
The flesh is bruckle, the fiend is slee:
Susanna's elders are on the spree.
The bailie beareth the belle away.
The lily, the rose, the rose I lay.

An interesting feature is the personification of Edinburgh as a sexual object which bears comparison with Sydney Goodsir Smith's 'The Black Bull o Norroway' which 'recounts his alcoholic and amorous adventures and misadventures among the publicans and sinners of Leith Street and culminates in an astonishing vision of Edinburgh personified and engaged to the act of perpetuating her existence by the most personal means'.[6]

The images of fecundity in this poem have a precedent in

Henderson's earlier work:

Lie alongside me, put your ear to the ground
and listen: the earth locks with fruitful adventures
And listen: the sap rises—sweet springs of song
like hymns of belief to the buds that will blossom.
My brother, no wails and no sterile revolt!
Tell the words from the depth,
Tell the fragrance above us
For soon, very soon, we shall harvesters be.
A lark in the skies show are those from darkness.
In happy embrace we shall hear in the dawn
You sowers of dreams, the crops have now ripened.[7]

They belong to a tradition of lyric poems and songs common in eighteenth-century Scottish literature that celebrates Spring counterpointed often with images of sexuality.[8]

Of course, the opposite of these images of burgeoning life are the images of death which also appear in Henderson's later poems in which 'the quick and the slaw are game for a tear… '

In what is possibly his last poem, the dead are again realised:

Under the earth I go
On the oak-leaf I stand
I ride on the filly that never was foaled
And I carry the dead in my hand[9]

And yet, is the poem just about death? Tom Munnelly comments: 'This poem is most emphatically not a valediction but a paean to the continuity of life which Hamish, like Joyce, has celebrated frequently in his work'.[10]

In 'The Flytin' o' Life and Daith', Henderson takes an old theme, the flyting, which can be found in Scottish and German medieval literature but reconstitutes it in a strikingly creative way. In keeping with his philosophy and instinct, it is, of course, love and life that triumphs in the end:

Quo daith, the warld is mine.
Your rantin' hert, in duddies braw,
He winna lowp my preeson wa'
Quo daith, the warld is mine.

Quo life, the warld is mine.
Though ye bigg preesons o' marble stane
Hert's luve ye cannae preeson in
Quo life: the warld is mine.

Quo daith, the warld is mine.
I hae dug a grave
I hae dug it deep,
For war an' the pest will gar ye sleep.
Quo daith, the warld is mine.

Quo life, the warld is mine.
An open grave is a furrow syne.
Ye'll no keep my seed frae fa'in in.
Quo life the warld is mine.

I suggest that if you take 'Floret Silva Undique' and 'Auld Reekie's Roses' – add 'The Flyting o' Life and Daith' (for which three separate tunes have been employed) as a sort of chorus (and perhaps also 'Under the Earth I Go') – then you have the bones of an epic poem or song sequence: a scenario of life, love and death played out against a background of contemporary Edinburgh. Also, there seems to be a continuation in this series that exemplies Ransford's four characteristics of Henderson's poetic work: 'pilgrimage, love-energy, integration, companionship'. Here is another typical sequence from 'Auld Reekie's Roses':

Day empty day advances
Gives lightsome dawn the lie.
The wayside pulpit calls us
To seek our joys on high.

The brothel-banks are open—
They cater for all needs.
The fozy voyeurs gather
To watch how money breeds.

But when the fun-fair opens
And bairnies ride the range,
The Oriental Gambler
Will snitch their smallest change.

Lay the lily O
O lay the lily O

Wake up then Camerados
It's time to make a move.

You can't be aye beach-combing
On lucky shores of love.

The brothel-bank's for busting,
The inmates all set free.
The Kirk, that dour dissembler,
We'll brak its back in three.
This seely Earth's our Salem
To Hell with Kingdom Come.
If Sergeant Death struts near us,
We'll slash his painted drum.

The wayside pulpit's dredgy
Can soond for ither lugs.
The joys o' Heaven we'll leave til
The angels - and the speugs.

Lay the lily O
O lay the lily O

Thomas Crawford notes that: 'Love and death are inextricably bound together in this refrain, for a lily can be a girl and 'lay' can mean fuck; at the same time, lilies (particularly arum lilies) are used in funerals; and to 'lay low' also means to defeat or 'ding doun'.'[11]

Throughout this sequence, in a series of almost surreal images, Henderson conjures up, against the backdrop of the old town of Edinburgh (around his home and Sandy Bell's) a Bacchanalian revelry of striking contrasts. Thomas Crawford notes the debt the poem pays to the famed 'Caledonian antizysygy' and comments:

> The kimmers o' Coogate are intentionally drawn from Sydney Goodsir Smith, whose own bohemian vision of 'the auld rortie city' is one of the poem's inspirations; and then we have the Deil who must be paid (from Burns and Dunbar), Death (called by his medieval nickname of 'Sma-back') snooving from his lair in the graveyard and, as additional correlatives of mental division, 'Janus guisers' coming out of the' darkmans' (an obsolete cant term used by Joyce in *Ulysses*). These scarecrow junkies, facing towards life and also towards death, are the down-and-outs from the Grassmarket; they are also zombies – the dead from the Greyfriars tombs. From their equally repellent dens on the opposite side come the prosperous Calvinist hypocrites, and both sets of folk dance Death's dance, with a direct reminiscence of Dunbar ('The flesh is bruckle, the fiend is slee'). But the poet's last word is again with life – with triumphant sex and fruition, summed up by a reference to an anonymous poem of the early sixteenth century – 'Flora is quene of lusty May'.[12]

So the awakening of Spring is yet again coupled with splendidly lusty orgiastic imagery and a lyricism in the tradition of Goliardic song and also reminscence of 'Polwarth on the Green' and other eighteenth-century Edinburgh poetry in the style of Ramsay and Fergusson.

I believe that in the later poems set in Edinburgh, Henderson was able to both employ an established style and a tradition of writing about Edinburgh, combining the folk idiom with a broader poetic perspective to create a new and distinctive voice.

There could have been a poem to rival Robert Fergusson's 'Auld Reekie' or Sydney Goodsir Smith's 'Kynd Kittock's Land.' But there wasn't. The promise was not fulfilled, and what we have is merely the skeleton of what might have been. Appendix One contains these three poems.

It is worth considering, therefore, to what extent does Henderson belong in a tradition of the poetry of Edinburgh. If I have glibly titled the unwritten complete poem of Henderson as 'Auld Reekie', it therefore bears comparison with Robert Fergusson's 'Auld Reekie'. Fred Freeman notes that, 'Henderson thus uses multiple literary voices, and a very unhomogenous variety of language and literary register to present a Fergussonian vision of 'Reekie'… which reconciles all its disparate elements.'[13]

Ferguson's 'Auld Reekie' was inspired by Gay and Swift and is in general more sedate than Henderson's version which also follows in the more Rabbelaisian tradition of Thomas Urquhart, William Dunbar and Sydney Goodsir Smith. In this sense, Goodsir Smith's 'Kynd Kittocks Land' and 'Gowdspink in Reekie' are comparison pieces. Alexander Scott sees them as: 'very like the mediæval Edinburgh of Dunbar [in which] characters dance skeleton like in the limbo between shadow and substance'. He also notes that: 'most of Goodsir Smith's Edinburgh poetry is nocturnal… The poet – like the 'reid tod' of one of his lyrics – comes out only after dark, when the douce burgesses who inhabit the cities daylight world are all safely abed'.[14]

Henderson's 'Auld Reekie' enlists both the daylight and the dark and can be seen, perhaps, to exemplify the infamous 'Caledonian antisyzygy' or the duality that is constantly identified in Scottish literature as a Gothic trend originating, most notably in James Hogg's *Confessions of a Justified Sinner* and Robert Louis Stevenson's *Jekyll and Hyde.*[15]

Finally, regarding the weightiness of Hamish Henderson's poetic output, it has neither the depth or longevity to compare with MacDiarmid or contemporaries such as Iain Crichton Smith or George Mackay Brown, but it a significant corps of work which can be seen to follow in a long tradition of Scottish and, latterly, Edinburgh, poetry.

References:

1. Regarding this see Fred Freeman, 'A New Voice on the Carrying Stream', in Eberhart Bort (ed.) *At hame wi' freedom: essays on Hamish Henderson and the Scottish Folk Revival* (Ochtertyre: Gracenote, 2012), p. 115.

2. Tessa Ransford notes, referring to an interview with Peter Orr, 'Henderson acknowledges the influence of Eliot in the *Elegies*, of Whitman too, and even Kipling undoubtedly, but he also acknowledges German poets whom he had read before the war, such as Rilke, Heine and Hölderlin. He states: 'If any poems have directly influenced my *Elegies*, I think it is the poems of Hölderlin and especially the later poems, the poems of his madness. In a time of tremendous suffering and war, small wonder that poems of a poet's personal suffering, horror, ecstasy and extreme agony should influence another poet.' Tessa Ransford, 'Encompass the Cross Sword Blades: Hamish Henderson's Poetry', in Eberhard Bort (ed.) *Born on the Carrying Stream: the legacy of Hamish Henderson* (Ochtertyre: Grace Note Publications, 2010), pp 137-160.

3. Tessa Ransford, 'Encompass the Cross-Sword Blades: Hamish

Henderson's Poetry', in Eberhard Bort (ed.) *Born on the Carrying Stream: the legacy of Hamish Henderson* (Ochtertyre: Grace Note Publications, 2010), pp 137-160.

4. Hamish Henderson, *Alias McAlias: Writings on Songs, Folk and Literature* (Edinburgh: Polygon, 1992), p. 54.

5. Tessa Ransford, 'Encompass the Cross-Sword Blades: Hamish Henderson's Poetry', in Eberhard Bort (ed.) *Born on the Carrying Stream: the legacy of Hamish Henderson* (Ochtertyre: Grace Note Publications, 2010), pp 137-160.

6. Alexander Scott, 'Sydney Goodsir Smith: the art of devilment', *Akros* (10th May 1969), pp 21-28, p. 24.

7. Unpublished poem from the Henderson notebook. Timothy Neat, *Hamish Henderson: a Biography, Volume 1: The Making of the Poet (1919-1953)* (Edinburgh: Polygon, 2007), pp 175-176.

8. See in this respect *Thomas Crawford, Society and the Lyric: a study of the song culture of eighteenth-century Scotland* (Edinburgh: Scottish Academic Press, 1979).

9. Hamish Henderson, *Collected Poems edited by Corey Gibson* (Edinburgh: Birlinn, 2019) pp 343-344.

10. Note by the song-collector Tom Munnelly quoted in Hamish Henderson, *Collected Poems edited by Corey Gibson* (Edinburgh: Birlinn, 2019) p. 345.

11. Thomas Crawford, sleeve notes for the album *Freedom Come-All-Ye, the poems and songs of Hamish Henderson* (Claddagh, 1977).

12. Thomas Crawford, sleeve notes for the album *Freedom Come-All-Ye, the poems and songs of Hamish Henderson* (Claddagh, 1977). A recurring opposition is between sexual freedom and Calvinistic oppression. Neat notes that 'Floret Silva Unique' was originally a poem written when Henderson was at Moray House in the late forties to '[rage] against these self-selected, life-hating, censorious teachers and their Calvinist doctrines'. Timothy

Neat, *Hamish Henderson: a Biography, Volume 2: Poetry Becomes People (1952-2002)* (Edinburgh: Polygon, 2007) p. 190.

13. Fred Freeman, 'A New Voice on the Carrying Stream', in Eberhart Bort (ed.) *At hame wi' freedom: essays on Hamish Henderson and the Scottish Folk Revival* (Ochtertyre: Gracenote, 2012), pp 109-130, p. 12.

14. Alexander Scott, 'Daylight and the Dark: Edinburgh in the poetry of Robert Ferguson and Sydney Goodsir Smith', *Lines Review*, 3 (Summer 1953), 9-13.

15. This set of oppositions is often overstated, particularly with respect to Gothic literature. The Edinburgh poet and magazine editor Craig Gibson states this robustly:

Duality, duality!
The sad inevitability!
For when'er debates arise,
With regard to the Scottish psyche,
Much talk of dualism,
Is highly fucking likely!

THE SONGS

Henderson said that he 'had come to set greater store by my songs… than by other kinds of poetry I have tried to write'. However, supposing he had a relatively sparse output as a poet (which we have seen to be only partly true) then the same is true, even more so, of his songwriting. The fact is that, although a few of his songs have wide currency, he actually only wrote thirteen discernible songs. Compare this to his contemporary, Ewan MacColl, who composed more than two hundred songs in his career.

One feature of his songs is the diversity of tunes he set them to. Here is a list:

tune	song
'A highland air'	Love Song
O We're Rusty Bums	Pioneer Ballad of Section Three
Solomon Levi	The Ballad of Gibson Pasha
Farewell to the Creeks	The 51st Highland Division's Farewell to Sicily
Lili Marlene	Ballad of the D-Day Dodgers
The Lincolnshire Poacher	Ballad of the Taxi Driver's Cap
The Gallant Forty Twa	Ballad of the Banffies
Bonny Glenshee(?)	The John Maclean March
Johnston's Motor Car	Ballad of the Men of Knoydart
Whistle O'er the Lave O't	Song of the Gillie Mor

The Bloody Field of Flanders	The Freedom Come-All-Ye
Viva la Quince Brigade	Rivonia
Which Side Are You On	Auld Reekie's Roses

The variety of tunes is clear: American Irish, English and German origin as well as Scottish. Henderson clearly had a good ear for a tune. Although it is a truism, a great song is a merger of words and music; which doesn't mean that they both have to be independently successful, it means that they have to fit together.

Generally, the triumvirate of the three great songs that Henderson penned are taken to be 'The 51st Highland Division's Farewell to Sicily', 'The John Maclean March' and 'The Freedom Come-All-Ye'. All three are reproduced in full in Appendix Two. I would be inclined to add the 'Ballad of the D-Day Dodgers' to these three. However, Henderson never claimed that he wrote it himself, preferring to attribute it to the war-time folk tradition. Stylistically, it is undoubtedly his work. Tessa Ransford notes: 'Charming as is the tune and sentiment of 'The 51st Highland Division's Farewell to Sicily', the 'Ballad of the D-Day Dodgers' is succinct and deeply satirical with its refrain of 'Italy', turning it to pathos in the last verse, entirely Henderson's composition, with the last line: 'Those are the D-Day Dodgers who'll stay in Italy' – because they 'slumber on' beneath 'the scattered crosses' on the mountains, 'some with no name'. The poem, as poem, is memorable and irresistible in its magnetism.'[1]

The rhetorical turn at the end of the 'Ballad of the D-Day Dodgers' when the satirical impulse of the rest of the song turns to a more sombre recognition of the reality of war, is one of the most effective and moving passages in all of Henderson's songs and poetry. 'The 51st Highland Division's Farewell to Sicily' as a song, however, is more than just 'charming'. John Mitchell has analysed this and other songs by Henderson:

> The first thing that strikes one is the surprising dialectical movement of mood in the lyric, the juxtaposition of two apparently opposite attitudes to Sicily. In the first four lines the feelings of human attachment and of repulsion, of 'not being at home' are inextricably interwoven. It all cuts two ways. Is the piper bored and home-sick? Or is he sad at parting? He is both. Is the sky over Messina uncanny and grey because it is an alien sky – or because it too seems to mourn the moment of parting? Both are involved. In the three 'choruses' which follow the first verse the negative aspect detaches itself and becomes dominant. This is reversed in the second verse and choruses, where the mood of estrangement melts into a deep human attachment to Sicily and its people. In the final chorus the Scottish troops seem to play a last salute to the mountain island on the instrument which symbolises their own national pride... Contrast it with the traditional songs of farewell, of leaving one's country for ever, in which Scottish lyric poetry is so rich ('Lochaber No More,' 'Farewell to Fuinary', etc) and its significant advance, its modernity, is obvious.[2]

It is, I think, the sense of a place and a time that makes this song so effective. It takes place in somewhere that is specifically located in history – a certain time during a long gone war. Yet it seems both immediate and universal. Mitchell notes, 'It is a grey eerie, inimical, inhuman place reminiscent of the 'cold hill-side in Keats's 'La Belle Dame Sans Merci', a place where man feels a stranger an *alien*, yet at the same time (and this is the important and final triumphant aspect). Behind the mask it is the world, the place where alone man's destiny is forged, where love and laughter and brotherhood will triumph over alienation.'[3]

The song evokes a time and a place which we do not have to be personally familiar with to appreciate. The same is true of 'The John Maclean March'. Simply reading this text gives no sense whatsoever of the power of the song, with its emphatic chorus and repetition of the first verse at the end. It evokes a Glasgow of shipyards and tenements. It may not be obvious, but the journey into Glasgow, along the Clyde terminating in Springburn, is symbolically the route that heavy industry took, taking the coal and iron to the steelworks and then the locomotive factories at Springburn, and back again to transport steam locomotives across the world. Thus, the song reflects the lives of the working people John Maclean championed. Again the tune is important to the song and, if I have a criticism, it is only because it may now seem, after the decline of the old Glasgow, a little too nostalgic and sentimental at times.

Finally to 'The Freedom Come-All-Ye'. This song has been a great success, yet it is an enigma. It is undoubtedly a poem-song a bit more than it is a song-poem and some aspects of it are, initially not easy to grasp. Henderson claims it was written in his native Perthshire Scots. Yet the very opening, 'Roch the wind in the clear day's dawin/ Blaws the cloods heelster-gowdie ow'r the bay', with its rhetoric inversion and language – which is more reminiscent of MacDiarmid's 'plastic Scots' – is neither colloquial nor, at first, easy to grasp. Also, if the language is difficult, then some of the concepts are more so: the move from the specific (Henderson wrote it on a train while watching the clouds) to the general 'the great glen o' the world', the condensed history, the references to Maclean and Springburn, all make it a complex and difficult piece.

Finally he ends the two last verses with non sequiturs:

> Black and white, ane til ither mairriet,
> Mak the vile barracks o' their maisters bare.
>
> And a black boy frae yont Nyanga
> Dings the fell gallows o' the burghers doon.

Clearly, the juxtaposition of the second last line with the last in either case can only be understood if we again can bridge the gap between the general and the specific, the international and the national, so that the connection between multiculturalism and the end of racism and the immediate circumstances in Scotland becomes manifest.[4] Corey Gibson comments on the last line here ' …the former colonial subject is the one to strike the final blow against the machinery of the bourgeois state. This hopeful vision of a revolution of the moment of rupture, international yet imagined from and through Scotland, is the highest example of this earnestness and idealism that cuts through in Henderson's best poems and songs.[5]

Yet, can it really be that this is an easy concept to grasp for the first time reader (hearer) of the song – in 1960 or, indeed, sixty years later? I suspect not. In fact, the song itself is an expression of a particular world view that has a historical context. Gibson summarises this:

> …it is perhaps the most compelling example of his conception of a party that "becomes people'. Written in 1960, and often associated with his CND campaigning (it was recorded for the *Ding Dong Dollar* record in 1962) the song combines contemporary international causes with a dense framework of Scottish historical and geographical references. The opening stanza's warning: "there's mair nor a roch wind blawin / Through the great glen o' the warld the day', also reads as revolutionary fervour: a great sea change in history swelling up beneath the speaker, the audience and their times. The Great Glen, that separates the Grampians from the Northwest Highlands, becomes a symbol of global division. And some commentators have interpreted the 'roch wind' as a reference to Harold Macmillan's Winds of Change" speech, in which the Tory Prime Minister appealed to the emerging nationalist movements in Africa to choose the path of the 'Free World' over that of Communism.[6]

The politics and the world concept writ throughout the short song make it a much more intricate and conceptual piece than might first appear.

Yet, despite all these difficulties that one might think would make it too complex a song for general consumption, it has been a massive success. David Stenhouse notes, 'It was sung in France during the 1968 student uprisings and later at devolution meetings and political protests in Scotland during the 1980s. At countless shivery rallies and rain-soaked marches, the 'Freedom' warmed up frozen throats. It was sung at the launch of the Scottish Constitutional Convention, where it chimed with Canon Kenyon Wright's declaration that 'we are the people and we say Yes'. It was sung at vigils and fund-raising ceilidhs… '[7] Despite all the difficulties and complexities the song presents, it has been adopted as a sort of alternative national anthem. Mitchell notes that 'The Freedom Come-All-Ye' points one significant way forward out of the dilemma in which contemporary British poetry finds itself, and it does so because it builds on the culture of the people.'[8]

This tradition becomes bound up not only with the popular nuclear disarmament movement of the sixties but also with a tradition of Nationalist and Republican sentiment and folksong exemplified by some of the popular 'Student's Songbooks' and by a publication which ran to two volumes in the 1950s: *The Rebels Ceilidh Song Book*:[9] ' …this wee Book of Patriot Songs, claiming no scholarly accuracy, seems yet to hold the spirit of authentic Scotland. Its songs, ranging from 'Stirling Brig' to 'The Haughs of Cromdale', show also our great sea traditions. It contains as well, a few industrial songs and some hauntingly beautiful Gaelic ones (some in translation) but all suitable for the youth of our nation, be they round the camp fire, or hosting in spirit with the Fingalians of old.'[10]

Apart from Henderson, it notably contains songs by Thurso Berwick (the pen name of Morris Blythman). Blythman, of course, was the progenitor of the *Ding Dong Dollar* songbook and album.

Another issue of the time concerns the private ownership of much of Scottish land that could be seen as the birthright of the Scottish people. One of Henderson's songs, from *The Rebels Ceilidh Song Book*, 'Ballad of The Men of Knoydart', commemorates a famous Highland 'land-grab'[11] It begins:

'Twas down by the farm of Scottas,
Lord Brockett walked one day,
And he saw a sight that worried him
Far more than he could say,
For the 'Seven Men of Knoydart'
Were doing what they'd planned—
They had staked their claims and were digging drains,
On Brocket's Private Land.[12]

An interesting comparison is Ewan MacColl's well-known 'Manchester Rambler', which again serves to lay claim to the outdoors on behalf of working class people, in this case, ramblers:

I've been o'er the Snowdon, I've slept upon Crowden,
I've camped by the Wain Stones as well,
I've sunbaked on Kinder, been burnt to a cinder,
And many more things I can tell.
My rucksack has oft been my pillow,
The heather has oft been my bed,
And sooner than part from the mountains,
I think I would rather be dead.

MacColl was present at the great mass-trespass that took place in April 1932 in protest at the denial of access to parts of the hills to the general public.[13]

It is relevant to end a discussion of Henderson's songs with a direct comparison with MacColl, both of Scottish parentage and both songwriters inspired by the folk tradition and socialist principles. Temperamentally unlike each other, they were friends but never particularly close. Their commonality was in the ability to join a tune, traditional or inspired by tradition, to a transcendental song that catches the spirit of a place or a time but makes it somehow universal and timeless.

The poems/ songs of *Auld Reekie's Roses* have already been mentioned, but I should also mention *Rivonia*, that great anthem to Nelson Mandela, not least because the melling of a Spanish Civil War tune with a contemporary political situation (1965) again demonstrates a superior facility with words and music.

To the question of the quality of Henderson's small but exceptional corp of songs, the only conclusion can be that the complex but striking integrity of the songs themselves shine through. Despite the small contribution Henderson made to songwriting, he did manage to create songs that have lasted the test of time and become a popular part of a new 'tradition'.

Yet how popular are they? Fred Freeman writes:

> Folksong (folk art generally), I am afraid, still has a lowly status in Scotland. [Few] have taken up Burns's challenge: 'those who think that composing is Scotch song is a trifling business – let them try'.
>
> Schools and universities may be 'developing new courses' in Scottish literature, but, beyond quick settings of the 'Skye Boat Song' and bastardized arrangements of a few of Burns's songs, there is no awareness of, for example, Tony Cuffe or Rod Paterson who have a grasp of eighteenth-century style and articulation, let alone the works of the great songwriters of today. Every child in this country should

> know 'John Maclean's March'… they should be familiar with the innovative pipe compositions of Gordon Duncan; The subtle orchestrations of Billy Jackson, Alan Reid, Donald Shaw and so many others. The sad fact is that they do not have probably never will. Now is the time for a rewakening. The 'hotbed of genius' is with us a germinating well though too much of it is too far underground in its native soil.[14]

Written around twenty years ago, Freeman's 'hotbed of genius' is a comparison with the Scottish Enlightenment of the eighteenth century. Can the period at the end of the twentieth century, during which Henderson created his most notable songs, be seen as as fruitful? Can his songs continue to have the relevance they had then? These questions impinge on wider issues regarding Scottish culture that will be addressed later in this study.

References:

1. Tessa Ransford, 'Encompass the Cross-Sword Blades: Hamish Henderson's Poetry', in Eberhard Bort (ed.) *Born on the Carrying Stream: the legacy of Hamish Henderson* (Ochtertyre: Grace Note Publications, 2010), pp 137-160.
2. John Mitchell, 'An Analysis of the Poetic Elements in Hamish Henderson's Songs', *Chapbook*, Vol. 3, No. 6, (ND), 7-23, 16-17.
3. John Mitchell, 'An Analysis of the Poetic Elements in Hamish Henderson's Songs', *Chapbook*, Vol. 3, No. 6, (ND), 7-23, 17
4. 'The last two lines with their introductory 'And,' are not an afterthought. They pick up and clarify dramatically the concluding two lines of the preceding verse. In smashing down the grim gallows of imperialism, the black boy from the other side of the world is

smashing the yoke of the burghers, the bourgeoisie – the enemy of communism in Springburn. The 'and' brings the thoughts of the fifth and sixth lines and those of the seventh and eighth into unusually close relationship; they emerge as two complementary sides of the same simultaneous whole. Thus, through the medium of art, the brotherhood, the individuality, the single complex identity of progressive man the world over, ceases to be a high-sounding abstraction, a phrase, and takes on a concrete, vital, significance.' John Mitchell, 'An Analysis of the Poetic Elements in Hamish Henderson's Songs', *Chapbook*, Vol. 3, No. 6, (ND), 7-23, 23.

5. Hamish Henderson, *Collected Poems and Songs*, edited by Corey Gibson, (Edinburgh: Polygon, 2019), p. xxx.

6. Corey Gibson, *The Voice of the People: Hamish Henderson and Scottish Cultural Politics* (Edinburgh: Edinburgh University Press, 2017) p. 152.

7. David Stenhouse, 'Scotland's Internationale', *Sunday Herald* (7th November, 1999), 11. My personal best memory of a rendition of the song is of Henderson on stage in Edinburgh on a bitterly cold night celebrating the release of Nelson Mandela.

8. John Mitchell, 'An Analysis of the Poetic Elements in Hamish Henderson's Songs', *Chapbook*, Vol. 3, No. 6, (ND), 7-23, 23.

9. William Kellock (ed.) *The Rebels Ceilidh Song Book*, Vols 1 & 2 (Bo'ness Rebels Literary Society, Bo'ness, ND). Numerous other small song books of contemporary songs in the folk tradition come out in the sixties. For examples Matt McGinn, *Scottish Songs of Today* (Harmony Music, London, 1964); Jim McLean, *Scottish Rebel Songs* (Socialist Review Publishing Co, Glasgow, 1968); John A Brune, *The Roving Songster* (Gillian Cook, London, 1965). Regarding these see Ewan McVicar, *The Eskimo Republic: Scots political folksong in action, 1951 to 1999* (Linlithgow: Gallus, 2010).

10. William Kellock (ed.) *The Rebels Ceilidh Song Book*, Vol. 1 (Bo'ness Rebels Literary Society, Bo'ness, ND), p. 25.

11. In 1948 The 'seven men of Knoydart', returning servicemen,

occupied land belonging to Lord Brocket, a known Nazi sympathiser, invoking the Land Settlement Act. Against a tide of public opinion, their claim was rejected by the Scottish courts. See Iain Fraser Grigor, 'The Seven Men of Knoydart: the story of one of the last Highland land grabs' in Billy Kay (ed.) *The Complete Odyssey: Voices from Scotland's Recent Past* (Edinburgh: Polygon, 1996), pp 71-78.

12. This song was written to the tune of *Johnson's Motor Car*, and was recorded as such by Hamish Imlach. However, it was later set to a tune specially written by Andy Roberts. See *Chapbook*, Vol. 2, No 5 (ND) and *Chapbook*, Vol. 3, No. 6 (ND), p. 35.

13. MacColl noted that he wrote three songs about the mass-trespass, although two seem to have been forgotten. Ewan MacColl, *Journeyman* (Manchester: Manchester University Press, 1990), p. 343. Also see Dennis Gray, 'A Drop of the Hard Stuff!' *Loose Scree* 33 (September 2006) 28-32, 29 and Simon Thompson, *Unjustifiable Risk: the story of British climbing* (Milnthorpe: Cicerone Press, 2011), p. 129. The desolate reaches of Kinder Scout and Bleaklow, in particular, attract some of the hardiest outdoor-lovers. When this song was written, these two great moorlands, Kinder and Bleaklow, were still privately owned and kept exclusively as grouse-shooting preserves'. Peggy Seeger (ed.) *The Essential Ewan MacColl Songbook* (New York: Oak Publications, 2001), p. 370. Also worth mentioning is MacColl's great elegy for a dying mountaineer, *The Joy of Living*, written in his seventh-second year after he had failed to climb Suilven. See Peggy Seeger (ed.) *The Essential Ewan MacColl Songbook* (New York: Oak Publications, 2001), pp 372-373.

14. Fred Freeman, letter to the *Scotsman*. See also Catriona M M Macdonald, *Whaur Extremes Meet: Scotland's Twentieth Century* (Edinburgh: John Donald, 2009).

FOLKSONG IN SCOTLAND

It has already been clear that more poems and songs of the standard Henderson was capable of would have been welcome. However, there is one more substantial missing piece of his life's work, or perhaps, the work that could have been. In the 1970s, at the height of the folk revival, Fred Woods notes: 'The high priest of Scottish folk studies, though, is Hamish Henderson... Hamish's discoveries in the field of Scottish folk music are almost legendary, beginning as they do with the towering figure of Jeannie Robertson and proceeding by way of Jimmy MacBeath, the Stewarts and Willie Scott, to name only a few. His written work on the subject, however, has been lamentably small so far.'[1]

What most of those involved in folksong sought from Henderson when we first grew to know him was some sort of statement on Scottish folksong. In fact, not just a statement, but a major work. What seemed to be wanting in the heyday of the Scottish folk revival was a *Folksong in Scotland* to rival Bert Lloyd's magnum opus *Folk Song in England*.[2] Who could have been better to write it? Henderson's experience of every area of Scottish folksong was immense (unusually, he also spoke Gaelic and understood the Gaelic tradition).

It did not, however, happen, and we can only piece together what Henderson might have written from the pieces he did publish, mostly found in *Alias McAlias*. In what ways, then, would Henderson's book differ from Lloyd's? There are, I think, some significant ways, which may, I suppose, inform a new 'history' of folksong in Scotland:

Lloyd's treatise is, in many ways a Marxist treatise, in

which folksongs are seen as workers' songs and as a dynamic underground counter-culture. Whilst Henderson would see some parallels, I believe that he would want to look at the interaction of folksong with society and to see how it might work in different cultural, political and technological contexts.

Lloyd dedicated a great deal of time, especially in his radio programmes in searching for similarities in international folk cultures. Whilst Henderson would be ideally equipped to do so, I believe he would also wish to identify what was distinctive about Scottish folk culture. He was well aware of the significant differences, for example, between Scottish, Irish and English folksong.

Lloyd takes a Marxist view of history which is itself politicised through this. I believe Henderson had an integrated view of history as a more fluid narrative that creates its own meanings.

Lloyd was, of course, writing in the aftermath of the first English folk revival, created by Cecil Sharp et al, who had constructed and written about the folk tradition in England. Henderson would have wanted to review the Scottish folk 'revival' of the same period which, of course, didn't really happen, despite the work of Gavin Greig and others. Henderson would also, I think, as a collector, take much more of an interest in the collectors and editors of folksong and how they constructed their own meanings.

Lloyd was more interested in the texts and histories of songs than the singers – at least on an individual rather than occupational sense. Henderson would foreground the carriers of the tradition, the farm labourers and travelling people.

Henderson would probably have far more to say about the

language (or languages) of folksong and its form (formulaic or otherwise) and mode of transmission.

Finally, Lloyd is interested in bawdry and the underground of folksong, but Henderson would probably emphasise it more.

These are assumptions, but we can also look at some of Henderson's actual publishing contribution to folksong scholarship.

Henderson's contributions to *Tocher*, the periodical reporting the work of the School of Scottish Studies, on individual songs and folktales were substantial, but the two most notable essays that he wrote in respect of the Scottish song tradition in general were "'At the Foot o' yon Excellin' Brae': The Language of Scots Folk-song" and 'The Ballad and Popular Tradition to 1660'. The first has already been considered in relation to the Scots language, but both also touch on the classic ballads, or 'muckle sangs' – a particular interest of Henderson's, and both demonstrate, I believe, a sophisticated and scholarly understanding of the fluid nature of the ballad text.

Henderson had, in fact, intervened in a particularly important debate regarding ballad studies. The Aberdeen scholar David Buchan had examined some Scottish ballads in a seminal study called *The Ballad and the Folk*.[3] Buchan underlines the key point of Albert Lord's epic study of Serbo-Croatian ballad singers: 'Lord has rendered much of our current terminology obsolete or ineffectual… Standard terms of literary criticism, such as 'author' and 'original text', and of folkloristic criticism, such as 'transmission', have vastly different meanings in oral and literate contexts.' Furthermore, he argues, our traditional concepts of literary criticism are rendered redundant in face of the sheer scope of the process of oral transmission and he emphasises the importance of this: 'a mature traditional singer can hear a story of perhaps some thousands of line once, and can thereafter re-tell the story at even greater length. The literate mind boggles[!]'[4]

However, one aspect of Buchan's study was seriously flawed and was been challenged by various scholars – not only Henderson and also the Danish scholar Flemming Andersen. It was Buchan's contention that a well-known ballad informant of the eighteenth-century, Anna Gordon (Mrs Brown of Falkland) was an examplar of the re-creation process. In fact, it has been demonstrated that she was literate and probably re-created texts she had read as well as heard sung. 'A subtle but significant distinction militates for the exclusion if those ballads for which Mrs Brown is the only source. If she had been illiterate, her versions – even though unique – would not have brought into question… but she was quite literate and often sang… with the text in her hand.'[5]

This was an important intervention by Henderson in the debate about the orality of the ballads, which is an ongoing debate. One scholar who took up many of the concerns and ideas expressed by Henderson in his work on the ballads (including some of Buchan's ballads and Jeannie Robertson's 'Son David') is David Atkinson, who has recently produced the most important and original study of the ballads for some time, *The Anglo-Scottish Ballad and its Imaginary Contexts*. Atkinson notes:

> The 'imaginary' in the title of this volume is quite deliberate. The ballad and its imagined contexts, with its echoes of Benedict Anderson's imagined communities, Georgina

> Boyes's imagined village, and Eric Hobsbawm and Terence Ranger's invented traditions, might have evoked an oral, ballad-singing community of a kind that owes as much to the broad thrust of Romanticism as it does to a historical back-projection from (limited) evidence drawn from the folksong revivals of the twentieth century. The imaginary contexts of the title, in contrast, refer to the abstract ideas that are the necessary counterpart of any attempt to describe the ballad – be it at the level of genre or of the individual literary/musical item in its social and historical context... The Anglo-Scottish Ballad represents the distinctive contribution of ballad studies to editing theory. In short, the ballad 'type' is identified as the abstract sum of all actual and possible manifestations, or 'versions', of what is recognizably the 'same' thing. The definition is notably circular – but it does mostly work in practice because there turns out to be a high level of seemingly inherent stability in ballad narratives and melodies, which makes it possible, most of the time, to recognize quite intuitively which items belong together.

Atkinson examines the nature of ballad of the fluid text and considers how and where it exists and what authority valids texts or palimsests. As he states, ballads can be identified 'intuitively' but their validation otherwise as a material form of literature is more complicated. I see this as a development of many of the ideas mooted in embryo form by Henderson.

I don't know if I am correct in my speculation on Henderson's possible impetus in the area of folksong and ballad studies in Scotland, and perhaps I have emphasised my own preferences and prejudices. However, I think that we can identify Henderson's main concerns in his corps of work on Scottish folksong and also a manner in which any future 'Folksong in Scotland' could be approached. However, eschewing speculation on what is not yet written, the final section of this study concentrates on the legacy of Henderson's life and work.

References:

1. Fred Woods, *Folk Revival: the rediscovery of a national music* (Poole: Blandford Press, 1979), p. 83.

2. A L Lloyd, *Folksong in England* (London: Panther, 1969).

3. David Buchan, *The Ballad and the Folk* (London: Routledge and Kegan Paul, 1972).

4. David Buchan, *The Ballad and the Folk* (London: Routledge and Kegan Paul, 1972), pp 51-52.

5. J Barre Tolkien, 'An Oral Canon for the Child Ballads: Construction and Application' *Journal of the Folklore Institute,* 4 (1967), p. 83. See also Andersen, Flemming & Pettitt, Thomas, 'Mrs Brown: a Singer of Tales?', *Journal of American Folklore*, 92 (1979); Henderson, Hamish, 'The Ballad, the Folk, and the Oral Tradition' in Cowan, Edward J (ed.) *The People's Past* (Edinburgh: EUSPB, 1980), pp 69-107.

6. David Atkinson, *The Anglo-Scottish Ballad and its Imaginary Contexts* (Cambridge: Open Book Publishers, 2014), pp xiii-xiv.

LEGACY

REVIVAL

The folk revival in Scotland of the mid 50s through to the mid 80s was itself a substantial movement. By a 'movement' I mean a movement akin to the hippie movement ore the punk movement. And by that I mean it was not just a musical phenomenon but also a distinct set of practices and beliefs with historic and socio-political concepts embedded in it.

When did the folksong revival begin? Henderson himself suggested that it began with the publication of *Ballads of World War II* in 1949.[1] However, another suggestion may be that it began with the Ceildihn in the Oddfellows Hall in Edinburgh as part of the 1951 People's Festival:

> The veteran Barra singer Calum Johnston again sang splendid Gaelic songs and played the pipes; the famous Lewis sisters Kitty and Marietta MacLeod enthralled the audience with 'Cairistiona' and 'Agus Ho Mhorag; an excellent bothy ballad singer from the North East called Frank Steele sang 'Come All Ye Lonely Lovers'; the young Arthur Argo, great grandson of the famous Aberdeenshire folksong collector Gavin Greig, sang 'The Souter's Feast' in a boyish treble; 18-year-old Blanche Wood sang songs she had learned from her aunt Jessie Murray; and Jimmy MacBeath gave of his best with 'Come All Ye Tramps and Hawkers' and 'The Moss o' Burreldale'… The singing began at 7.30pm and finished, rather hilariously, about two o'clock in the morning. It was an event of incalculable importance, because from it sprang a hundred other fruitful cultural enterprises in subsequent years. Instead of 'Muckin' the Byre' in white tie and tails

and Kelvinside accents, there was the glorious singing of Flora MacNeil and Calum Johnston from the Isle of Barra, John Strachan singing the classic ballads 'Clyde's Water' and 'Johnnie of Breadislee', the artistry of Jessie Murray, a Buckie fish-wife whose incomparable 'Skippin Barfit Throw the Heather' [was performed].

Attracting people who felt excluded by the International Festival, keeping the admission prices low and including children – it was Gramsci in action! One of the things that attracted me to Gramsci was his great interest in popular culture. He was a Sardinian, and the Sardinian folksong is rich and bountiful and vigorous to the nth degree. When he was in prison he wrote to his mother and sisters asking for details about their folk festivals. Gramsci in action was the People's Festival.[2]

Also in 1951, Henderson had been introduced to Alan Lomax by Ewan MacColl and that summer they both undertook a recording trip around Scotland which partly resulted in one the of earliest folk albums, *Heather and Glen*. This was before Henderson became a full-time member of the School of Scottish Studies in 1952

So the folk revival was clearly established before the flytings with MacDiarmid began in 1959. The Edinburgh University Folksong Society was formed in 1958 and through the 1960s folk clubs sprung up throughout Scotland including Aberdeen where Arthur Argo published the first folk magazine, *Chapbook*. Argo promoted folksong on BBC radio whilst, in Glasgow, Norman Buchan and Thurso Berwick promoted folksong in schools and Drew Moyes established the Glasgow Folk

Centre. In 1962 the 'Ding Dong Dollar' collection of songs was published followed by *The Rebel Ceilidh Song Book*. The Aberdeen Folk Festival was the first of many such as the annual festivals held by the Traditional Music and Song Association in Kinross and Newcastleton.

This is a simplification of the range of events involving a variety of different contributors. But can it be easily pigeon-holed? Fraser Bruce, one of the best known musicians and club organisers of the time, who has been studying folk clubs and their participants during the period, has a different view:

> You will have picked up on the fact that I don't believe there was a revival. I believe that the songs were being sung locally but were not recognised as 'folk' songs. To most, including the Travellers, they were songs that could be mixed up with Hank Williams, Harry Lauder and laterally, The Beatles.
>
> It is great that Hamish Henderson, Ewan MacColl and Alan Lomax did what they did, but few people realise that there were others such as Seamus Ennis and Peter Hall out there collecting as well.
>
> [Many people] made a contribution to folksongs over the centuries, including the people and musicianss that were creating a 'folkscene' in the 1950s/60s and 70s. However, I want to eradicate the belief that it was one man who created it all. I will not destroy the general beliefs about Hamish Henderson but simply highlight that there were others involved. Indeed, at no point in any of the books that I have read recently does Hamish Henderson make any claims of greatness. He is extremely generous in complimenting other contributors.[3]

However, Henderson was instrumental in the development of folksong collecting in Scotland. His contribution as a collector of the folk tradition is almost unrivalled and he did it the hard way, living in travellers' tents, getting to know the people, coaxing their life stories out of them. Yet he did not alone construct the Scottish folksong revival and it has too often been too easy to accept that he did.

So, whilst giving Henderson due credit for his work, it is not the case that Henderson 'discovered' the Scottish folk tradition on his own. Perhaps I am nitpicking, but I don't like the word 'discover' very much. Timothy Neat likes to use it, in one instance with reference to the 'Horseman's Word'. Henderson used the term also. He often claimed to have 'discovered' Jeannie Robertson, the great Aberdeenshire ballad singer (he identified that as his proudest achievement). However, there is a little dubiety about that too. Timothy Neat suggests that William Montgomerie recorded her songs before Henderson did.[4]

There is something, I suppose, that, over a period of time, has made me feel a little uneasy about the figure of Jeannie Robertson. Am I alone in thinking that there is something strange about a folk movement that stresses the democracy of its tradition and, simultaneously, the residence of that tradition within a non-hierarchical common folk, promoting just one singer to the role of high priestess?

Henderson had fought for some time to try to get folksong on the BBC. He believed that the poet and producer George Bruce (possibly in league with MacDiarmid) contrived to keep folksong off the air. Something had to be done – the control had to be wrested from an establishment that promoted 'high culture' and the wider aims of capitalism. Jeannie Robertson provided that opportunity, as her growing fame allowed her singing to be broadcast (and made into commercial recordings). She *had* to become a figurehead, I suppose. The cost of that, paradoxically, is that Jeannie once again is seen as a 'discovery' – as something precious and unique in herself rather than as an example of the wider tradition of the Scottish folk tradition and the hundreds of other singers who keep it alive.

Now Jeannie is gone, as are most of the other 'informants' of the heyday of field recording, but folksong still exists. So it is fair to ask, if Hamish Henderson was the progenitor of the folk revival, how does it stand without him?

Of course, the end of the revival has been presaged on many occasions. By myself, in 1988: 'I think it is important to be aware that the folk revival, which supported academic research into the folk tradition by, to some extent, piggy-backing it on the successful social milieu of the folk club/scene, has rather died a death (although folk music is still widely performed: it may be, as Ian Watson puts it, that we have witnessed the 'general decline' of the folk club in all parts of the country coupling with an increasing absorption of the more easily digestible end of the folk scene into the commercial context and festival circuit of pop). The end of the revival era was, in fact, proclaimed at an important conference held in 1986 in County Hall, London, the headquarters of the GLC, to celebrate the seventieth birthday of Ewan MacColl, at which various ageing stalwarts from both the academic and the folk club arena met to reminisce and to reassess the role of the folk movement in the light of the New Age.'[5] Strangely, I remember that many of the participants at the event seemed rather old –

Ewan MacColl, Peter Kennedy, even Henderson – but that is something that has not changed. A few years ago, at a concert for MacColl at Glasgow Caledonian University, I was possibly the youngest of about one hundred guests. Similarly, folk clubs have notably aged members.

Yet, if folksong is entering a new age, there is still a lot of it! We used to eagerly await any new recording or song book or the weekly release of the *Sandy Bell's Broadsheet* or *Scotia Folk*. Now there are countless recordings of folksong and numerous publications about it. Even back in the 1980s there seemed to be a new age in folksong. I wrote: 'My primary impression in looking back at the folk scene of the early seventies is rather nostalgic but… it is the impression of a distinct identity – of belonging. In retrospect, the strange elitism… the feeling that folksong is somehow going to change the lot of the common man, seems blatantly ridiculous… the ultimate paradox is that a social group that often seemed insular, complacent and self-congratulatory should so clearly identify itself with an oppositional culture – a radical socialist perspective concerned with the celebration of common sympathies…'[6] So, are things better or worse than they were then? Is the spirit of the folk revival still alive or is folksong now just another form of commercial entertainment? I am genuinely unsure.

In my own area, the study of folksong, there has been a profusion of academic work but it has (perhaps like much work on the humanities) trended towards the safety net of specialisation rather than inter or multidisciplinary approaches to the folk tradition within a wider network. In the 1980s, journals like *Cencrastus* could run folksong articles side by side with pieces on the Scottish cinema or critiques of tartanry and kailyard. But that urge towards a more multi or inter-disciplinary version of Scottish cultural studies seems to have died (or has it – were wider questions of national and cultural identity not raised in the first referendum debate, and was folksong not included in that?)

My problem is that I am probably yearning for something similar to what, I think, Henderson sought, a more cohesive cultural, social umbrella for what I would like to call Scottish Studies. I suspect that is no longer possible because of changes in society and disciplinary structures.

So what is the way ahead? The unified folk revival movement failed because it had intrinsic internal inconsistencies. It was based on flawed and not always compatible discourses – 'the imagined village', 'red Clydeside', etc. And the longing (or, if you like, the hope and the promise) that the folksong revival was founded on, for a unified set of beliefs that merged our quest for a personal, cultural and national identity, that explained the communal past experience of working people and offered a philosophy, quasi-political, that transcended the mundane world of capitalism. It was a project that was doomed to fail. Part of the problem of the cult of Hamish Henderson is the problem with the folk revival in general. It is too easy to romanticise the past, to learn the sacred litany: Hamish Henderson, 'The Freedom Come-All-Ye', Jeannie Robertson, 'My Son David', Matt McGinn, 'Ding Dong Dollar', etc, etc.

I have a radical solution to this problem. That is to forget Hamish Henderson – by which I don't mean forget him personally, but I do suggest that, rather than enact annually the usual rather banal tributes to him, we could instead direct our energies to some of the issues that would still absorb him if he were alive: for example, how does the Scottish folk tradition construct our concept of local and national identity? What is the relationship between folksong and popular or 'high' culture? How does the folk tradition fit into the wider political agenda in post-referendum Scotland?

These are the sort of questions that a more contemporary folk revival might pose. The revised edition of Ailie Munro's *The Folk Revival in Scotland* is titled *The Democratic Muse,*[7] taking a nod from *The Democratic Intellect* by George Davie. Could this suggest a more general form of revival – a revival at the centre of a nationwide form of renaissance that typifies perhaps what is different about Scotland and Scottish national identity within its context in the wider United Kingdom.

Paradoxically, after the failure of the devolution referendum of 1979 to engender a more independent Scotland, there was an upsurge, something like a new Scottish rennaissance, in the 1980s. New studies of Scottish history and literature were published; journals such as *Cencrastus* were founded; Angus Calder, Tom Hubbard and Tessa Ransford inaugurated the Scottish Poetry Library. Cairns Craig notes that, 'Revivalism was the median by which Scotland's difference and distinction was continually reasserted through the years of the incorporating Union that ought to have made Scotland an indistinguishable part of the cultural polity of the United Kingdom'.[8]

So next I shall consider to what extent the folk revival still plays a part in a developing sense of a Scottish national culture and identity.

References:

1. Hamish Henderson, 'Tangling with the Langholm Byspale', *Cencastus* 48 (1994).

2. Hamish Henderson, "It Was In You That It A' Began: Some Thoughts on the Folk Conference' in Eward J Cowan (ed.) (Polygon: Edinburgh, 1980), pp 13-14.

3. From an unpublished manuscript.

4. Timothy Neat, *Hamish Henderson: a Biography, Volume 2: Poetry Becomes People (1952-2002)* (Edinburgh: Polygon, 2007), p. 23.

5. Ian Spring, 'Folksong in Scotland: Image and Reality', *Cencrastus*, No 29, 31-33, 31.

6. Ian Spring, 'Folksong in Scotland: Image and Reality', *Cencrastus*, No 29, 31-33, 32.

7. Ailie Munro, *The Folk Music Revival in Scotland* (London: Kahn and Averil, 1984), republished as *The Democratic Muse: Folk Music Revival in Scotland* (Aberdeen: Scottish Cultural Press, 1996).

8. Cairns Craig, *The Wealth of the Nation: Scotland culture and independence* (Edinburgh: Edinburgh University Press, 2018), p. 30.

THE CARRYING STREAM

The title of the celebration for Henderson organised by the Edinburgh Folk Club after his death was 'The Carrying Stream'. This clearly suggests a continuation of the folk tradition through oral transmission or otherwise. However, let's consider to what extent that is a valid metaphor. Fraser Bruce notes that:

> Arthur's grandfather, Gavin Greig, had written, in a paper presented to the Buchan Field Club in 1906-07, that 'our rural districts long ago, almost everybody sang or tried to sing. The standard of vocal entertainment was low, and no accompaniments were needed. The occasions were always social, and criticism was mild. Around the ingle, or in a barn where all were neighbours and cronies, nobody who could sing at all would hesitate to contribute his or her favourite ballad or ditty. Nowadays, we cultivate singing as an art, till, as a rule, in a company, nobody will sing at all unless they can do it fairly well.[1]

At the beginning of the next century groups such as the Traditional Song Forum[2] exist to promote traditional songs, but it is the case, noted by almost everyone involved in folksong, that folk sessions, ceilidhs, or most other avenues for the promotion of folk have become more instrumental rather than voice based, more elitist and more commercial. There has been a sea change in the environment for promoting folksong. When I first attended the Tradition Folk Club in Glasgow it was *de rigeur* that everyone had to sing, as in Ewan MacColl's Singers Club in London. That could not be imagined these days. Folk clubs have become more like concert venues and the Traditional Music and Song Association, once an avenue for informed comment on the Scottish folk tradition, has become more focused on the organisation of gigs or commercial events. I believe that these would have been unwelcome developments for Henderson

I have already suggested that two specific assumptions about Hamish Henderson's career are 'myths': firstly that he devoted his entire time to the folk tradition rather than his own writing; secondly, that he wished his own poetry to be preserved purely by oral transmission (rather than in printed form). To be absolutely clear, I am suggesting that these assumptions may be partially true, but are not absolutely correct, and need to be re-examined by any serious critic. They are stated by Raymond Ross, editor of his *Collected Poems and Songs*:

> With Hamish the refusal to go 'collected' – when I occasionally ask him about it – is always based 'officially' on the Folk Revival, on the work he's done – and is doing – in relation to the Travellers. 'I've put all my eggs in one basket,' he says at the back of Sandy Bell's. This is the party line and he always sticks to it. Then, he switches the conversation to the late, great Jeannie Robertson or calls on someone to give us a tune. The master deflector. He'll willingly give Jeannie her 'halo' (more than willingly, in fact); but he don't want no halo effect for himself. There's always that leftwards shuffle from the 'personal' to the 'collective'.[3]

This would seem to be supported by Henderson own statement: 'I have preferred to read poetry out, and if it is a song, to sing it. I am quite conscious of the fact that this immediate communication has got its own strong drawbacks. The audience cannot often grasp a thing immediately but nevertheless, this immediate communication, this immediate aural communication, has been to me personally of enormous interest'.[4] In a book review he summons up the Spanish poet Lorca to support this position: '[Lorca] consciously operated in an oral tradition, and mistrusted print… When his poems and plays were printed he considered them 'dead on the page', but when he read them to others he could make them live and protect them… ' He was essentially averse to committing himself to print. His literary friends had to use countless stratagems in order to extract a poem from him… '[5]

In fact, Henderson did not give up writing poetry when he started collecting songs or, indeed, when he started writing them. There are over one 180 pieces in Gibson's new edition of his *Collected Poems* and he wrote poetry over several decades. There is as much poetry by Henderson as there is by some other, more acclaimed, poets.

I have already posed the often mooted question: how is it that someone of Hamish's great ability and early promise could produce comparatively little of his own work and, a corollary, why is it that the work he did produce should engender so little in the way of critical acclaim, or even criticism?

Often an oppositional model is posited in answer to this question: Henderson'preferred' to work in the folk rather than the literary tradition because he found it more 'fulfilling', 'real', 'important' than pursuing his own career as a poet. Therefore, he made a conscious decision to concentrate on his collecting in opposition to his writing. I do not, in essence, believe that this true. Henderson, it has been revealed more recently, wrote a lot more poetry and prose than once appreciated (although there is still not a full bibliography of his work). He did this despite finding writing quite arduous, as he admitted to me. Nevertheless, I believe that he was well aware that there were many different avenues for disseminating his work apart from oral transmission. It is not often noted that he collaborated with Timothy Neat on a series of documentary films (and even appeared in a feature film). Also, he promoted the early recording of traditional songs on the Folkways and Topic labels and was even sympathetic to the incongruous guitar accompaniments which were insisted upon for the earliest of Jeannie Robertson's recordings.

Is the 'carrying stream', then, a thing of the past. Well, no, it can be seen to have been reconstituted in different forms. For a start, much more poetry is now being performed live, at regular meetings in pubs and clubs held by groups such as the Heretics in Edinburgh and The Cheeky Besoms in Glasgow (albeit some of it is focused more on the performance than the poetry, in, for example, the strange phenomenon of the 'poetry slam', a poetry performance competition).

Secondly, it cannot be seen as desirable that social media has taken over a lot of informal personal contact, but social media does offer a, arguably democratic, avenue for short performances, poetry, songs, opinions to be disseminated among groups of like-minded folk quickly and easily. New technology has an effect on the transmission of literature, culture and all the creative arts that cannot be understated and deserves a full length study in the context of the traditional arts.

Finally, another development in recent years that Henderson would presumably have welcomed is the renewed interest in the Scots language. As we have seen, Henderson took a creative view of Scots in his definition of ballad Scots: 'Scots may be said to include English and go beyond it' and notes that '[the question for Scottish poets] is not so much one of language as one of idiom.'

I think that Henderson, with this in mind, would quickly have identified some inherent problems with the current Scots language 'revival'.

Firstly, literary Scots, sometimes referred to as Vernacular, Doric or Lallans, has always been a contested area. At the beginning of the last century MacDiarmid had a public spat with the vernacular circle of the London Burns Club[6] regarding the suitability of Scots for modern poetry. Subsequently, his 're-invented' Scots was labelled 'plastic Scots' by Douglas Young.[7]. In fact, literary Scots comes in various forms: for example, what commonality is there between the work of William Dunbar, Sydney Goodsir Smith and Tom Leonard?

Secondly, Scots as a spoken language. The Scots Language Centre, an organisation set up from the A K Bell Library in Perth, claims just about every local dialect as Scots and posts examples on its website (this was first introduced, I think, along with census questions a few years ago): Glaswegian, Shetlandic, Aberdeenshire Doric etc. All these are legitimate forms of language, but to lump them together as 'a language' (a commonly shared system of communication) leads to the nonsensical conclusion that Scots who may well not understand *each other* are speaking the same language.

What would be Henderson's attitude to these developments? Well, I think he would have defended the spoken work as inherent in the voice of Scottish people and would have shooed away attempt to shoehorn Scots into a new framework.

For Henderson, Gibson suggests: 'Folk culture becomes a framework for tracing the interrelatedness of of Scotland's languages and its literature and folk-art. Scots language is only as distinguishable from English as folk-poetry is from art-poetry'.[8] This, simply, is a view of the 'carrying stream' in action.

References:

1. From an unpublished manuscript.

2. Tradsong.org.

3. Raymond Ross, 'The Tombstone and the Halo', in Steve Byrne (ed.) *The Hamish Henderson Papers* (Edinburgh: The Hamish Henderson Archive Trust, 2013), pp 53-62.

4. Hamish Henderson, *Alias McAlias: Writings on Songs, Folk and Literature*, (Edinburgh: Polygon, 1993), p. 325. From an interview with Peter Orr. My memory may be selective, but although I remember Henderson singing I can hardly remember an occasion on which he recited his own poetry live.

5. Hamish Henderson, *Alias McAlias: Writings on Songs, Folk and Literature*, (Edinburgh: Polygon, 1993), pp 313-314. He is quoting J L Gili.

6. For more on this see Mary Symon, *Collected Poems* (edited by Ian Spring and Fred Freeman), (Perth: Rymour Books, 2020).

7. Note also that MacDiarmid's own poetic Scots was not always accepted even by other Scots poets. Lewis Spence comments "Theirs [MacDiarmid and followers] is an artificial lingo, not found on the lips of the people, nor written on their hearts'.

8. Corey Wilson, *The Voice of the People: Hamish Henderson and Scottish Cultural Politics* (Edinburgh: Edinburgh University Press, 2015), p. 189.

If we examine some of the mythology surrounding Hamish Henderson, it can be seen that one of its most significant components is nostalgia This nostalgia is two-fold. Firstly, a nostalgia for a lost history, lost in the sense that few of us remember it directly – a history little recorded in the annals of establishment history, relying to some extent on memory and oral history.

Secondly however, is a nostalgia for the era in which the instrument of nostalgia, for example, a song, was written or performed. This is the most potent form of nostalgia because it is often a nostalgia for something that never actually existed or was imagined. A key text in understanding the folksong revival is title *The Imagined Village*.[1] In that study, Georgina Boyes considers how the folk revival in England created an imaginary, synecdochal and idealised view of a past that exists outside of established history or politics.

Probably the two best known songs written by Henderson (and certainly the most often performed) are 'The John Maclean March' and 'The Freedom Come-All-Ye'. Regarding the first, there is no doubt that this is an example of the 'hero song' par excellence. Hearing it performed by Arthur Johnson, the Glasgow singer, is impressive and moving The second is a more complex song but also purveys the same sentiment and notably features Maclean.

Maclean has become a potent symbol of a socialist and nationalist Scottish workers movement. Yet the complexity of the politics of the period of what was called Red Clydeside are seldom addressed. Iain McLean considers the height of the movement and concludes that it is a legend more than a reality and marshalls fairly convincing evidence to suggest that the political impact to these events was severely limited:

> On 31st January 1919 – 'Bloody Friday' – a vast demonstration of unofficial strikers in front of the City Chambers in George Square was very roughly broken up by the police, and the next day six tanks lay in the Saltmarket with their guns pointed at the citizens of Glasgow. In the 1922 General Election, Labour won ten out of the fifteen seats in Glasgow, and the new MPs, several of them colourful leftist rebels, were given a tumultuous send-off from St. Enoch Station: The singing of 'The Red Flag' was general. From these famous scenes, and many others like them, springs the legend of Red Clydeside. It is a powerful legend, which entranced many in its own time and has continued to do so ever since. It records how Clydeside was ripe for revolution throughout the First World War; how the revolution just failed to occur in January 1919; and how some of the revolutionaries entered Parliament four years later, still determined to wipe capitalism out. It is a stirring story, which impressed frightened members of the 1918-22 Coalition Government as much as it did the revolutionaries themselves. Nevertheless, it is a legend.[2]

It was the time of a European Communist démarche with the Russian Bolsheviks, the French Army Mutiny and the German revolution. But the revolution never materialised in Scotland.[3]

Therefore, in 'The John Maclean March', Maclean's symbolic march back to Glasgow after his release from prison is a surrogate triumph that achieves its effect through a potent nostalgia. The similar apotheosis in 'The Freedom Come-All-Ye' ('When MacLean meets wi's freens in Springburn/ A' the roses and geans will turn tae bloom') can also be seen as a form of wish fulfilment.

However, these are songs and they are fictions – fully permitted to indulge in nostalgic sentimentalism. In a wider sense, the problem with nostalgia is that it distances cultural and political theory from present-day concerns. I addressed this dilemma some time ago: 'To deny the political importance in these terms of Red Clydesideism, however, is not to disparage it. At worst, it presents a particularly inspiring set of myths. It is oppositional, which is no bad thing, but mythology is endlessly reconstructed according to the tenor of the times. However motivating the legend of John Maclean may have been at the right time, in the right place, it falls oddly flat in today's ideological climate. This is partly because it is recuperated through nostalgia, partly, because it is a myth of community [while traditional communities are under threat]'.[4]

The cultural appropriation of the legends of John Maclean (or, for example, the Calton martyrs) to address current political and cultural issues is not invalid but it is problematic.

Henderson was not, of course, unaware of the limitations in real political terms of the use of sentiment or nostalgia. The play *Krassivy,*[5] by Henderson's friend Freddy Anderson, takes an entirely uncritical view of John Maclean and, to an extent, exaggerates his achievement (It was Maclean who prompted James Connolly to organise the Irish Easter Rising of 1916). However, Henderson always took a more nuanced view of political events than Anderson. When, in 1987, Anderson published a collection of his poems – *At Glasgow Cross and other Poems.*[6] It is often thought that Anderson over-valued some of his political poems. Before the volume was published, Hamish Henderson wrote to him on this matter suggesting that he ditches one intended poem, *The Red Herring*:

> The latter—in my opinion—is too simplistic and 'overstated' even to make an effect as propaganda. I'm all in favour of hard-hitting polemic poetry, but it *has* to have a 'dialectical' element in it. Most of Europe political poems are too dualistic for my liking: they say 'we're right and they're wrong'. Nobody—no reader of poetry, at any rate—really believes this. The complexities of life are too great. Alright, I'm 100% against Thatcher and Reagan—and have tried to show it—but that doesn't mean that I don't see blemishes… on the Russian side.'[7]

In his otherwise effusive introduction to the collection, Henderson hints at this unease: 'Some may consider his world-view too perfervid to take in, and put into focus, all the deep paradoxical complexities of our present human situation on this beleaguered planet.'[8]

I have already detailed Henderson's view of Calvinism as an oppressive stifling and life-destroying force within Scottish culture. This is a view echoed in recent times by a multitude of Scottish writers and intellectuals. In fact, according to most accounts, Scotland is a profoundly *sick* nation! The pathologies of Scotland are numerous and a full taxonomy would occupy more space than is available. However, some of the most mooted pathologies can be stated as follows.

Firstly, there are the phobic disorders that encompass not only anglophobia and the oft-quoted 'kent-yuir-faitherism' but also the general results of inferiorism noted above which, in their most potent manifestation – as outlined by Craig Beveridge and Ronald Turnbull in *The Eclipse of Scottish Culture*[9] – become a sort of second-order of signification, afflicting the critics and academics who try to define the discourses themselves. Also included can be the 'Scottish cringe' and various manifestations of inferiority as outlined, for example, in Carol Craig's *The Scots Crisis of Confidence.*[10]

Secondly, there are the schizophrenic disorders – the oft-quoted Caledonian Antisyzygy, a term coined by Gregory Smith, a sort of reconciliation of opposites commonplace, seemingly, in Scottish literature These are often also articulated in oppositional metaphors of Scottish history and literature such as 'dark and light', 'heart and head' (as I have identified in respect of the Edinburgh poems).

There are the depressive disorders, often expressed in an elegaic discourse (regarding, for example, the evacuation of St Kilda or the Highland clearances) which is a sort of version of the Celtic Twilight and a longing for a lost golden age seen in, for example, the literature of Edwin Muir or Fionn McColla. On the contrary, in urban represenations, depression often reveals itself as what has been called miserabilism.

The most discussed, however, of these pathologies, often cited as an endemic sickness at the heart of Scottish identity, is displayed in a body of theory which again derives from a continental influence. Based on the work, notably, of Michel Foucault, it tries to identify different discourses that typify Scottish popular culture. Several discourses have been identified and some are more relevant to Scottish urban culture, for example, the discourse of Clydesideism (a form of Workerism) and the so-called 'Scotland on the move' discourse (a form of modernism). However, the two most often quoted – and arguably essential – discourses, that are usually referred to in tandem, are tartanry and kailyard – Scottish versions of the wider traditions of romanticism and sentimentality.

Both of these terms, tartanry and kailyard, have a more substantial pedigree, but their critical introduction is generally dated to two crucial critical interventions in the development of Scottish cultural criticism – the Scotch Myths exhibition of 1982, organised by Barbara and Murray Grigor, and the Scotch Reels event of the same year and the subsequent collection of essays published under the same title and edited by Colin McArthur.[11] These important cultural interventions occur in parallel with some of the important work of Henderson through the School of Scottish Studies.

So how does the work of Henderson fit in with these pessimistic manifestations of Scottish culture? The easiest way to approach that problem is through his views on what he called 'the enemies of folksong'. As Gibson puts it:

> Henderson describes these 'enemies' as an 'élite' who, in countries with a pronouncedly stratified class structure, 'invariably have their work cut out when trying to come to terms with their own folk-culture'. In Scotland the problem is exacerbated by the fact that 'the élite are to a big extent also the elect, and consequently have a vested interest in keeping the songs of the damned well battened down under hatches'. Conflating the terms of class politics and

> Scotland's Calvinist inheritance (the 'elect and the damned'). Henderson imagines folk-song's enemies dwelling in every sphere of cultural, social, political and spiritual influence...[12]

Henderson himself states:

> The elite, especially in countries with a sharply stratified class-structure, invariably have their work cut out when trying to come to terms with their own folk-culture. The trouble here in Scotland has been, and still is, that the élite are to a big extent also the elect, and consequently have a vested interest in keeping the songs of the damned well battened down under hatches. Firmly entrenched in all key positions of administration, religion and the organisation of culture, the elect deny just as long as they are able that anything so vulgar as popular culture exists.[13]

On one level he is referring to the opposition to his own work at the School of Scottish Studies, but in general there is an ongoing theme in his work. Popular culture, folksong, the voice of the people, whatever you call it, is a sort of healing balm that salves the damage caused by distorted, bowdlerised and repressive products of the Calvinist establishment.

If we take it, then, that tartanry and kailyard produce sentimentalised or warped impressions of Scottish nationhood, then it is to the authenticity of folk culture that we have to look for a correlative. This is certainly a view expressed not only by Henderson and it was a key tenet of the movement known as the Folk Revival.

Finally, let's consider Scotland as an imagined nation. This concept is not new. Benedict Anderson's study of nationalism, *Imagined Communities*, offers the now well-established definition of a nation as 'an imagined political community… imagined because the members of even the smallest nation will never know most of their fellow-members, meet them, or even hear of them, yet in the minds of each lives the image of their communion.' In Anderson's terms, 'a nation is never so ancient, so established, or so clearly defined as it is imagined to be in the eyes of even the most moderate nationalist.'[14]

It is tempting to compare the fluid nature of national identity to Henderson's understanding of the fluid nature of the ballad text. Both can be easily realised in a single manifestation, but their definition is much more difficuly upon consideration. Gibson notes that Henderson, ' …recognised the arbitrariness of the 'nation' yet chose to work within a national framework'.[15]

Of course, the problems inherent in imagining Scotland are manifold. Partly because of its unusual status as a 'stateless nation'. Its status also, of course, is predicated by the fact that it co-exists as a state with a larger and, arguably more powerful neighbour – what Paul Scott refers to as 'in bed with an elephant'! For Michael Gardiner the realisation of this relationship is, for a small nation like Scotland, always an ongoing process: 'I propose that we think of Scotland, borrowing the terminology of the French philosopher Gilles Deleuze, as a minor nation. For Deleuze… minor does not mean small or insignificant; it describes the function of iteration (speaking) working within a larger, major, language or power – here Standard English dialect or the British Empire – and it implies an entity that is always becoming something else. Scotland, in Deleuzian terms, always has to become in the face of a more powerful being, since, as a nation with no state, it has no official identity.'[16]

One consequence of this relationship is a resentment of the more powerful nation that can be exemplified in anglophobia. However, there is a more subtle and hegemonic consequence that influences the articulation of Scotland and Scottishness.

Of course, not only was Henderson well aware of these complexities but they were fundamental to his life and career. An international who had fought on the side of the Allies in the War, a Highland Scot who, nevertheless had studied at an Englsih public school and Cambridge. A critic of anglophobia who fought for the recognition of an independent Scotland.

With regard to Scotland's difficult relationship with England, there is a body of theory that derives from the concept of cultural imperialism. It fits into two categories with similar resulting conclusions. Firstly, that which employs the work of anthropologists such as Claude Levi-Strauss and Jack Goody and is best expressed in a Scottish context in the work of Malcolm Chapman[17] who typifies the Celtic Fringe as imagined in terms of romantic qualities that are superficially attractive but, at heart, politically and ideologically disabling.This body of theory constitutes concepts of 'the other' through what is sometimes called 'the Grand Dichotomy' or 'Core/Periphery theory'. It often employs a set of oppositions and is expressed in general terms as the idea that the peripheral culture is constituted as a sort of inverted reflection of the dominant core culture. Secondly, derivations from the work of cultural critics such as Edward Said and Franz Fanon and the concept of 'inferiorism' – described by Craig Beveridge and Ronald Turnbull as 'those processes in a relationship of national dependence which lead the native to doubt the worth and significance [of his own culture] and embrace the styles and values of the coloniser'.[18] Ian Bell appropriates the eighteenth-century term 'scotticism' to explain this process of marginalisation: 'Only certain representations of Scotland seem authorised, and the occasions and styles of utterance are regulated by the gaze of power... Scottish sympathies are immediately stigmatised as wayward, enfeebling, and disabling. They prevent Scots and Scotticists seeing things in themselves as they really are.'[19]

Furthermore, there is an argument, expressed by Colin McArthur, that "Scottish cultural studies' is stifled or marginalised by the 'imperialist' influence of 'British cultural studies... if there is no lack of cultural studies in Scotland, why has 'Scotland' so seldom been the subject of study within it?[20] He points out that there is practically no reference to Scotland in most of the key texts on British cultural studies. His argument is that a (mostly Marxist) critique of cultural imperialism seems to drive disciplinary paradigms for the study of cultural experience in the English language but that it has not generally been applied to the the Scottish situation. In the more recent times, in Owen Jones's *The Establishment*, an important text in terms of the political state of the United Kingdom, only two pages refer to Scotland.[21]

However, the independence debate and the evolving political situation in Scotland is endendering a great deal of discussion on issues of national and cultural identity especially since it comes at a time of international political turmoil. Henderson lived through different forms of striving for Scottish independence, political or cultural, from the Home Rule movement through devolution to the establishment of the Scottish Parliament in

1999.

Although most of the rather abtruse theory summarised above was formulated during a period (the end of the last century) during which Henderson was active both as a collector and a writer, he did not directly engage with it. He told me on more than one occasion that he found it difficult and a distraction from his collecting and creative work. However, it is relevant as it constitutes an agenda for the further development of the debate on the nature of Scottish national identity and the possibility of Henderson's contribution to that debate. Corey Gibson points out that Henderson lacked the 'sure-headedness' of MacDiarmid and his egotistical and monolithic approach to the definition of the Scottish nation, but that can be seen as an asset in the current complex debate. Corey Gibson, in the last section of his deep, insightful study notes: 'Because of the range of Henderson's interests, and his largely anecdotal reputation, there is a risk that this 'legacy' may simply be that of a folk hezo on whom a range of political and cultural views can be projected [but] Henderson's place as a nexus for different political and cultural communities is well documented… On the basis of this detailed critical analysis of Henderson's writings, I think he may be more accurately and more usefully located.'[22]

The imagined Scotland of Hamish Henderson can perhaps be detected in the nostalgic revisitations of the red Clydesiders, the continued flyting between the repressive tropes of Calvinism and the liberating forces of the oral tradition of the people, the humanitarian ethos of his later poems. The question is, to what extent can it be re-mobilised in an ongoing and politically fraught discussion on the nature of Scotland and the Scottish people?

References:

1. Georgina Boyes, *The Imagined Village: Culture, Ideology and the English Folk Revival* (Manchester: Manchaster University Press, 1994).

2. Iain MacLean, *The Legend of Red Clydeside* (Edinburgh: John Donald, 1983), p. 1.

3. See Christopher Harvie, *No God and Precious Few Heroes: Scotlsnd, 1914-1980* (London: Hodder Arnold, 1981). The title is, of course, taken from a line in the *Elegies.*

4. Ian Spring, *Phantom Village: the myth of the new Glasgow* (Edinburgh: Polygon, 1990), p. 113.

5. Freddy Anderson, *Krassivy*: a play about the great socialist, John Maclean, Glasgow Caledonian University: Glasgow (2005). Reprinted in Freddy Anderson, *Collected Poems and Prose* (Perth: Rymour, 2020).

6. Freddy Anderson, *At Glasgow Cross and Other Poems*, Fat Cat Publications: Glasgow (1987).

7. Recorded in the Hamish Henderson Archive, University of Edinburgh and the Freddy Anderson archive, Glasgow Caledonian University.

8. Freddy Anderson, *At Glasgow Cross and Other Poems*, Fat Cat Publications: Glasgow (1987).

9. Craig Beveridge & Ronald Turnbull, *The Eclipse of Scottish Culture* (Edinburgh: Polygon, 1989).

10 Carol Craig, *The Scots Crisis of Confidence* (Colintraive: Argyll Publishing, 2003)

11. Colin McArthur (ed.), *Scotch Reels: Scotland in Cinema and Television* (London: British Film Institute, 1982). Note that I have summarised somewhat simplistically a complex area here. For example, Craig Beveridge and Ronald Turnbull are often seen as criticising the

arguments of Tom Nairn, Colin McArthur and Murray Grigor.

12. Corey Gibson, *The Voice of the People: Hamish Henderson and Scottish Cultural Politics* (Edinburgh: Edinburgh University Press, 2015), p. 167.

13. Hamish Henderson, 'The Enemies of Folk-song', in *Alias McAlias: Writings on Songs, Folk and Literature*, (Edinburgh: Polygon, 1993), pp 45-50, p. 46. Henderson is a good deal more circumspect than MacDiarmid in this respect, who refers to: 'the 'whole gang of high muck-mucks, famous fatheads, old wives of both sexes, stuffed shirts, hollow men with headpieces stuffed with straw, bird-wits, lookers-under-beds, trained seals, creeping Jesuses, Scots Wha Ha'evers… commercial Calvinists, makers of 'noises like a turnip' and all the touts and toadies and lickspittles of the English Ascendancy, and their infernal women-folk'.

14. Benedict Anderon, *Imagined Communities: Reflections on the Origin and Spread of Nationalism* (London: Verso, 1991).

15. Corey Gibson, *The Voice of the People: Hamish Henderson and Scottish Cultural Politics* (Edinburgh: Edinburgh University Press, 2015), p 209.

16. Michael Gardiner, *The Cultural Roots of British Devolution* (Edinburgh: Edinburgh University Press, 2004). More recently, Gerry Hassan, in *Caledonia Dreaming: The Quest for a Different Scotland* (Edinburgh: Luath, 2014) has identified Scottish myths that are more overtly political. These are his six myths of Modern Scotland:

The Myth of Egalitarianism

The Myth of Educational Opportunity

The Myth of Scottish Democracy

The Myth of Social Democracy

The Myth of Holding Power to Account

The Myth of Open Scotland

17. Malcolm Chapman, *The Gaelic Vision in Scottish Culture* (London: Croom Helm, 1978). An example I have written about in depth is

the representation of St Kilda. The circumstances of the St. Hilda's way of life and their subsequent evacuation from the homeland is described in terms that tend to distance it from more immediate concerns. Therefore those very circumstances are described as unique or lost in the past. this, of course, leads to the fact that the St Kildan's way of life was not unique and their problems were common in Highland Scotland in the twentieth century, and also that the problems encountered by the St Kildans are problems that's still exist in various forms for small and isolated island communities.

18. Craig Beveridge & Ronald Turnbull, *The Eclipse of Scottish Culture* (Edinburgh: Polygon, 1989).

19. Ian A Bell, 'Scotticism: Textual Attitudes and National Characters', *Southern Review*, Vol. 23, No. 2 (July 1990), 127-136, 127.

20. Colin McArthur, 'Some Musings on Scottish Popular Culture' *Cencrastus*, 28, x.

21. Owen Jones, *The Establishment: and how they get away with it* (London: Allen Lane, 2014).

22. Corey Gibson, *The Voice of the People: Hamish Henderson and Scottish Cultural Politics* (Edinburgh: Edinburgh University Press, 2015), pp 203-204.

It is interesting in itself that the most recently constructed celebration of Henderson, the Hamish Matters Festival in Blairgowrie, is based on a pun.

'Hamish Matters' of course, implies the matters of substance of the celebration that relates to Henderson. It also suggests however that 'Hamish matters' – is relevant to the contemporary world as exemplified by the celebration itself. So does Henderson matter? Of course he does as a person – someone we have loved and lost and who still lives on in our memories. But the larger question that arises is to what extent does Henderson's work, his ideas and his principles still matter or apply to the contemporary world, or to what extent does the political and cultural concepts developed by Henderson impinge upon current political and cultural situation?

To consider Henderson, his reputation and the continuation of his work today? I will begin with a small controversy. I was going to head this section *In the Hamish Henderson Archives*, after Janet Malcolm's well-known *In the Freud Archives*, a tale of skulduggery and deception. I am not quite sure if the story of the Hamish Henderson 'archive' is quite so murky. However, in order to avoid contention I will attempt to state the facts as I know them before continuing, in this and the next chapter, to evaluate the extent of Henderson's legacy; whether contained within his collected papers or the debate that his life and work has engendered.

Firstly, the Hamish Henderson Archive was initially, at least, only an 'archive' in the loose sense. Henderson was something of a hoarder and kept just about everything willy-nilly in the office or his flat. Tim Neat suggests that he envisaged his 'archive' when he was eight years old. This seems unduly precocious. In fact, I am not sure that Henderson saw his papers as an archive at all: he simply liked to keep things, like letters from those he knew. It was Timothy Neat who started to refer to an 'archive' when he reviewed the papers stored in the basement of the School of Scottish Studies after Henderson's death.

Secondly, if there is an archive, it is not a complete collection of Henderson's papers or possessions. After Henderson's death, the family arranged the sale of some of his more valuable possessions, largely through the bookseller Gordon Wright (although some unsold copies were returned to what now constitutes the Hamish Henderson Archive). Also, some of Henderson's papers were donated to or purchased by the National Library of Scotland. These are properly catalogued and can be found online.[1]

The rest of Henderson's papers were available for sale from the Henderson family; they had the papers valued by an Edinburgh bookseller and approached various libraries. Edinburgh University Library, I believe, baulked at the price assigned to them and other libraries weren't interested.

Subsequently, a third party, a well-known Scottish folksinger, using a social media site, set up the 'Hamish Henderson Archive Trust' in June 2011. The declared purpose of the Trust was to raise a sum (initially set at £2000, although more was donated) to help find a buyer for the Henderson papers ('archive'), 'valued at almost £100,000' from the Henderson family.

Eventually, the University of Edinburgh acquired, from the Henderson family via the Trust, a collection of Hamish

Henderson's personal papers. The University notes that it is by no means a complete collection of Henderson's accumulated papers, as there are others in public and private collections. The papers include some diaries and other material, but approximately sixty percent of the material consists of letters to Henderson. The University employed Excel spreadsheets provided by the Hamish Henderson Archive Trust to catalogue the collection. Initially, access to the archive was only as mediated through the archive librarian. The collection is various: since Henderson did not distinguish in his collecting of material, there are personal letters in the collection that have little scholarly value along with letters of some noted writers and scholars.[2]

Concerning the activities of the Archive Trust and their use of the considerable sums donated to them, the most tangible result, apart from their website, seems to be the inventory, as above, and the publication of a slim volume entitled *The Hamish Henderson Papers* amounting to some 66 pages.[3] The Hamish Henderson Archive Trust continued to exist after the purchase of the material, still seeking donations and advertising on its website 'Having fulfilled our main goal, the Trust continues to operate towards enhancing the public knowledge and understanding of the poetry, traditional culture and folklore of Scotland, particularly concerning the life and works of the poet, folklorist, and songwriter Dr Hamish Henderson'. Their stated ambitions to produce a web page which is 'the main internet resource' for Hamish Henderson, and an academic journal dedicated to his work, have not been realised.

To the best of my knowledge, The Hamish Henderson Archive Trust was not a charity and was not registered as such with the Office of the Scottish Charity Regulator or with Companies House and no accounts have ever been made public. Therefore, legitimate concerns have been raised about its accountability and availability for public scrutiny.

More importantly, are Henderson's papers now secured and a valuable resource for the nation? Well, according to some of the published rhetoric, the papers are a valuable treasure, important for the nation and for twentieth-century Scottish cultural history. In actual fact, a great deal of it has already been scrutinised and published, notably, in Timothy Neat's massive biography and in Alec Finlay's excellent edited collection of Henderson's letters, *The Armstrong Nose.* And more recently, by Corey Gibson as research material for his two important contributions to Henderson scholarship. It *is* a resource but it is difficult to estimate how important it is.

As noted above, by far the most significant recent intervention in 'Hamish Henderson studies' have been Corey Gibson's edited collection of the poems and his *The Voice of the People: Hamish Henderson and Scottish Cultural Politics.* Gibson diivides his study into the following sections:

The Flytings
War Poetry and Soldiers' Songs
Gramsci's Folklore
Poetry and the People
The Revivalist and the Folklorist

I have already touched on the flytings – which I tend to see as more a side product of the cultural revival than a progenitor of it – the war poetry and the folk revival, but I have said little about Henderson's relationship with the theories of Antonio Gramsci. Gibson notes that 'the Sardinian thinker is perhaps the figure most frequently invoked throughout Henderson's disparate writings'.[4] However, Gramsci does not appear at all in the published essays in *Alias MacAlias*, and references to him in *The Armstrong Nose* are slight and mostly from the letters to MacDiarmid arguing about the nature of the Folk Revival. Henderson translated Gramsci's *Prison Notebooks* over a period of time (MacDiarmid mocked him for his laxity); they were eventually published in 1959 but probably didn't achieve the detailed consideration they deserved at that time. Other Scottish intellectuals, however, were interested in the broader aspects of Gramsci's work, notably his theory of hegemony that had been adopted by Raymond Williams, Stuart Hall and the New Left. Gibson cites Angus Calder, Tom Nairn and Ray Burnett, for example. There is no doubt that Gramsci's political ideas were applied fruitfully to Thatcherite and Blairite Britain and that they could, in the contemporary situation, be applied to the political and cultural landscape of Scotland, the 'stateless nation', but that was not a part of Henderson's consideration. The section of the *Prison Notebooks* that Henderson referred to most was the section on folklore which amounts to only a few pages. This, and Gramsci's interest in the Sardinian language was the inspiration that fed directly into his views on language, folklore and folksong. Political theory was not something Henderson engaged with in relation to Gramsci. Gibson concludes: 'Henderson rarely appears even in the marginalia of critical material on Gramsci. In works on Henderson, on the other hand, Gramsci is given due recognition as an enormous influence in the development of his thought.'[5]

That is not to say, however, that Henderson's work is not relevant to the sontemporary cultural and political situation in Scotland. It can be argued that we now need is a cultural politics in which 'the voice of the people' can be more firmly stated and an ongoing political and cultural debate in which the minority and peripheral voices that Henderson championed can be foregrounded. How that is to be achieved in the 'post-truth' era is an ongoing question.

In a sense we have come circle in that what Henderson began his adult life fighting against has once again began to emerge. Citing the rise of such as Donald Trump, Matteo Salvini and Boris Johnson, Fintan O'Toole writes:

> To grasp what is going on in the world right now, we need to reflect on two things. One is that we are in a phase of trial runs. The other is that what is being trialled is fascism – a word that should be used carefully but not shirked when it is so clearly on the horizon. Forget "post-fascist" – what we are living with is pre-fascism… Fascism doesn't arise suddenly in an existing democracy. It is not easy to get people to give up their ideas of freedom and civility. You have to do trial runs that, if they are done well, serve two purposes. They get people used to something they may initially recoil from; and they allow you to refine and calibrate. This is what is happening now and we would be fools not to see it.[6]

One cherished goal of Henderson's, an independent socialist Scotland (a republic?), however, seems not so far-fetched as it did in his time. The ongoing independence debate and what has been called a 'conversation' with the Scottish people provides a forum for Henderson's work and ideas to be reconsidered and part of his radical agenda realised.

Through part of this study I have indicated that the uncritical adulation afforded to Henderson from some quarters is not helpful in a critical appreciation of his life and work. This is echoed in a more recent piece by Mairi McFadyen:

> Through the collective act of mythologising such a figure, there is a risk that the expansive world of Hamish Henderson becomes foreclosed and self-referential. The past can be a vital resource for the future, but too much nostalgia distracts us from the vital work – the darg – that we must do in the here and now, with an eye to the future. We must continually check our blind spots; Henderson had his blind spots too.
>
> The ground under our feet is shifting very fast. Right now is the time when the transformational change must begin. Indifference is not an option. To understand that we are always unfinished gives us radical hope that things can change, that poetry can 'become people.'[7]

'The Darg' (meaning daily labour) is also the title of a volume of poetry edited by Jim Mackintosh and published by the Poet's Republic Press in honour of Henderson on the occasion of the 100th anniversary of his birth.[8] Although only a slim volume, it was enthusiastically received and packed out a reading at the Edinburgh Book Festival. The intention of the volume according to the editor is to '[take] up the baton passed on by Hamish and those who shared his many causes. It might fairly be said that is the task – the darg – of the living, and of our times.' Many of the poems are tangential to that aim but some are interesting reflections on the man and his work.

Poems in Scots and Gaelic (by Sheila Templeton and Marca Mac an Tuairneir) envisage Henderson on the road with the travellers or singing in Sandy Bell's:

> …steerin oan
> ower roddies an tracks, traivellin the land
> in yer cairt an shaltie, spikkin tae aabody
> gaitherin the deep sangs o oor story
> birthed yirdit fae traivellers' throats…

> Ach an là sin, ann an Sandy Bells,
> bhriseadh ar rannan
> le guth cronnachadh…

Modern Clydeside is portrayed in the post-industrial era by A C Clarke:

> …where the redcoat fortress topping Dumbarton Rock
> peers over tidal flux, with the bored eyes
> of retirement, at Greenock's white boxes
> stacked tier on tier up the hill, at the docks
> where cranes twiddle their thumbs…

The legacy of the *Elegies* is confronted by one of Scotland's best poets, Hugh McMillan in a poem called 'Leaving Alexandria':

> …And so in history's boiling footprint
> we suffer: those who fought,
> those who heard the fighting,

those whose wars
were spawned on others…

And the fraught history of the Highlands is summed up by Neil Young:

I know what guidebooks do not tell:
anguish like a rash that runs
through scant, perfunctory lines,
famine years and palmed-out pay
that emptied half a country of men…

Of course, these were not the first attempts at poetry in honour of Henderson. Bob Bertram had written a poem for his funeral and, subsequent to that event, Henderson's ashes were scattered on a Perthshire hill. The event inspired Geordie McIntyre who notes: 'Gulabeinn (The Curlews/Whaups Mountain) lies to the north-west of Spittal of Glenshee. Hamish, with his mother, spent the first five years of his life in a rented cottage. He, with his mother, climbed to its 2645ft/806m summit at the age of four. To quote his friend and biographer Tim Neat, the mountain 'became a living presence to the young Hamish'. In May 2002, a party of four – son-in-law Charlie Marshall, Angus Calder, George Gunn and Tim Neat – trekked to the summit where a suitable 'natural tomb' was found to deposit Hamish's ashes. George Gunn was the ash bearer.'[9] This is the poem McIntyre wrote:

This mystic hill 'of youth and age'
Towers o'er the Fairy Glen

Banner-bright in May morn light
To welcome Hamish home.
From Glenshee to Sicily
A' the airts the winds do blaw
"Come gies a sang cried Seumas Mhor
Let the music flow
A song to cheer a weary heart
Ane to drive away dull care
Tales of comradeship and hope
That we all can share.
Rabbie Burns and Thomas Paine
Gramsci, Lorca, John Maclean
Listen to their clarion call
Let peace and freedom reign.
All the sacrifices made
Do not let them be betrayed
Raise your voices, stand as one
Is the song – from Gulabeinn.

Around the same time the Gaelic poet Donald Meek penned this tribute, simply title 'Seumas MacEanraig', or 'Hamish Henderson':

Hamish Henderson
A tall, tousled man
With the breeze of Blairgowrie
        on his breath
and the heritage of Glenshee
        in his soul;
standing as a tree-trunk

in the forest of the ages,
hearing the hunt
of Diarmad and the boar,
        the hounds cresting the hill
and Fionn sitting sulking
In the shade of Ben Gulbainn
He comes to mind
as I walk
among the knolls of the glen
the river soft murmuring
        under the stone bridge of Kirkmichael
the tale of Diarmad and Grainne
                and Hamish
as undying music in my ears.
        May he himself have peace
in the glen.[10]

Henderson, despite his many achievements, began and ended his career as a poet and it is, perhaps, with the poets that his legacy truly remains. Tessa Ransford notes:

> Hamish was in the midst of things all his life and desired that his poetry be life, become people. What could that mean? The phrase is borrowed from Heinrich Heine's statement that 'Freedom must become people'. Heine's statement in the 1830s that when books are burnt, people will be burnt too is inscribed in the Bebelplatz in Berlin where the Nazis burnt books in the 1930s. The phrase also reminds us of ideas from the Sardinian Communist thinker Antonio Gramsci about culture forming its own 'society' and

> affecting politics to the extent that it can almost be claimed that 'the politics follows the culture'. If we think about this we can see that it is true. Without a culture of service and subservience there can be no empire, and no mafia, for instance. Without a culture of poetic vision, creative thinking and steady building of infrastructures, there can be no freedom becoming people. There are individual people and there are groups of people, societies of people, communities of people, nations of people, the world of people. Poetry needs to be 'in the midst of things' in all these circles within circles – for the individual to individuate and live in hope, for the community to have vision, openness and freedom from fear, for nations to operate on principles of freedom, collaboration and acceptance of diversity rather than fear, prejudice and deterrence.[11]

The epithet 'poetry becomes people' is often used in reference to Henderson's work. It can be taken simplistically, as perhaps in the second volume of Neat's biography, to mean that Henderson turned his attention from the writing of poetry to the nurturing of people, or of poetry in people, but Ransford takes it more expansively to encompass a world vision in which the spirit of poetry, or creativity, is nurtured within people, or a people, or peoples to engender a vision for the present and the future. That seems a good summary of Henderson philosophy and the direction of his life's work.

References:

1. National Library of Scotland, AC 12643.

2. This fact prompted a curious contribution to the popular press: 'Some of the letters are incredibly mundane, but they are interesting for that reason – that they are showing us that revered tradition bearers… were just as ordinary as the rest of us. *Edinburgh Evening News* (8th August, 2013).

3. *The Hamish Henderson Papers*, edited by Steve Byrne (Edinburgh: The Hamish Henderson Archive Trust, 2013).

4. Corey Gibson, *The Voice of the People: Hamish Henderson and Scottish Cultural Politics* (Edinburgh: Edinburgh University Press, 2015), p. 77.

5. Corey Gibson, *The Voice of the People: Hamish Henderson and Scottish Cultural Politics* (Edinburgh: Edinburgh University Press, 2015), p. 80.

6. *Irish Times* (Tuesday 26th June 2018).

7. Mairi McFadyen, 'Hamish Henderson and the Liberated Life', *Bella Caledonia, (*published on 16th August 2019).

8. Jim Mackintosh (ed.) *The Darg* (Stonehaven: Poets Republic Press, 2019).

9. From the programme for the Carrying Stream Festival.

10. From the programme for the Carrying Stream Festival. Translated into English by Bill Innes. This is the original:

Duine ard craiceach
le oiteag Bhlar Ghobharaidh
        air anail
agus dualchas Ghlinn Sidhe
        'na anam;
'na sheasamh 'na chraoibh
ann an coille nan linntean,
's e ag eisdeachd ri faghaid
Dhiarmaid 's an tuirc,
        na gadhair ris an leathad
's Fionn 'na shuidhe gu gruamach
fo sgail Bheinn Ghulbainn.

Cuimhnichidh mi air
's mi a' coiseachd
am measg tulchain a' ghlinne,
an abhainn bhog ri monbhar
        fon drochaid chloiche ann an Cille Mhich-
's sgeulachd Dhiarmaid is Ghrainne
                is Sheumais
'na ceol biothbhuan nam chluasan.
        Gum biodh sith dha fhein
anns a' ghleann.

11. Tessa Ransford, "Literature must desire to be life, not an idea of life': Hamish Henderson's vision 'Poetry Become People", in Eberhard Bort (ed.), *'Tis (sic) Sixty Years Since: the 1951 Edinburgh People's Festival Ceilidh and the Scottish Folk Revival* (Ochtertyre: Grace Note, 2011). pp 159-165, pp 159-160.

COINCIDENCES

Having attempted to evaluate the nature of Hamish Henderson's legacy and contribution to Scotland's cultural history, I will indulge myself by concluding with some personal reminiscences.

My father and Hamish Henderson were born in Scotland only a matter of hours apart and both served in the desert and in Italy during the war (they might well have met) although their backgrounds were quite different: my father a working class factory labourer and Henderson a public school boy and scholar. Neither came from privileged backgrounds: Henderson from the small cottage in northern Perthshire; my father from the tenements of the Gorbals in Glasgow. Yet, despite this connection their lives followed very different trajectories. Henderson's career is well known, my father's not at all (although part of it is recorded in my first book)[1.] His life was lived in a room and kitchen in Dennistoun, Glasgow working in a paint factory. He died prematurely and sadly from a brain tumour in 1969 and his funeral was on my fourteenth birthday.

My own scholarly career was an exception for my own family and was influenced and shaped to a great extent by Henderson who I met at the age of 19 and who introduced me to and encouraged me in my interest in the Scottish tradition.

My interest in Scottish folksong had arisen from my final years at school, Allan Glen's in Glasgow. The school had a record of encouraging an interest in folksong. Morris Blythman (Thurso Berwick) had taught there, but before my time, and my sixth form teacher (a Mr Shearer) encouraged me to write a long essay on Glasgow children's songs. Schoolfriends took me to the Tradition Folk Club in the Bank Restaurant in Queen Street which was run by Jimmy Ross and Miller Frondigoun in the fairly strict ethos of Ewan MacColl's Singers Club in London. I soon recognised that my abilities were not as a performer (I wished they were!) but as a scholar, and, at an early age, I began collecting folksong and ballad books.

Some time in 1974. I had written to Henderson and he invited me to meet him at the School of Scottish Studies, as he did, I believe, in the case of all aspiring scholars who contacted him. That this meeting inexorably shaped my life is beyond question, as it set me off on a path of scholarship that constituted my subsequent academic life. Henderson seemed a reasonably old man when I met him, although he was younger than I am now. He was an imposing figure, full of enthusiasm, suggestions, ideas, gifts – and it was impossible not to become enamoured of him as everyone did. Dick Gaughan describes his first meeting with him:

> ...In the tiny back room of the White Horse Bar in Edinburgh's Canongate, just below the Netherbow... This impossibly long and gangly character who began to sing *The 51st Highland Division's Farewell to Sicily* in a voice which was cracked and thin, quite unmusical and distinctly military in presentation. To me, at all of 17 years old, he looked ancient and, as he flapped his arms, punctuating his delivery by waving his pint dangerously over his head, he looked like a puppet with a crazed drunk working the strings. Like most things to do with Henderson, it was slightly surreal."[2]

I knew Henderson quite well, but others, I'm sure, knew him better. I was only one of many notable folksong scholars he nurtured. I am not qualified to write about him, therefore, because of any particular insight I may have into his life and work. On the contrary, what I write about him comes from the point of view of one of many of his acolytes and one who is, probably, typical of many who knew him. And knowing Henderson wasn't always easy: you may have had to search for his dog on the Meadows, put him in a taxi, pay his bar bill when he had forgotten his wallet, pick him up when he stumbled or rescue him from someone he didn't want to see! He was not just a mentor, he was a complete person, roguish, lovable, unpredictable.[1]

The last time I saw Henderson was in a care home in South Edinburgh. I was living in Surrey at that time and I travelled up to visit him. A little while before I had been to the funeral of Henderson's friend, the Glasgow poet Freddy Anderson, and I told him of Freddy's death (strangely, I was the one who informed Henderson of the death of Hugh MacDiarmid (at the Kinross Folk Festival; I had heard about it on the car radio on the way there)).

It was on my birthday in 2002 that a friend phoned me from Edinburgh to inform me of Henderson's death. The funeral was held on 15th March 20002 in St Mary's Episcopal Cathedral in Palmerston Place.

At that time it had been my intention for a while to move back to Scotland as soon as it was feasible: either to Glasgow or to Edinburgh. After the funeral, surrounded by the classic architecture of Edinburgh's West End and New Town I decided that I would move to Edinburgh and, in fact, shortly afterwards I bought a property in Palmerston Place only a few hundred yards from the Cathedral. Another strange coincidence follows. I discovered that the flat I owned was the drawing-room portion of an Edinburgh townhouse once occupied by William McDowell. McDowell was a book seller and auctioneer in Edinburgh and historian, known for his history of Dumfries and a book on ballads. Furthermore, Henderson had encouraged my research into bawdy Scottish songs encapsulated in my annotated edition of Peter Buchan's *Secret Songs of Silence.* While researching that, I had been made aware of another manuscript of bawdy songs kept along with the Buchan manuscript in the collection of the Houghton Library at Harvard, *Jocular and Burlesque Ballads*, songs expurged from the published collection of James Maidment. However, at that time, it was not fully described in the catalogue. Subsequently, the catalogue was enlarged and I discovered, from a note regarding the provenance of the manuscript, that it had been purchased in the late nineteenth century from William McDowell, bookseller, Edinburgh. The address was that of my flat in Edinburgh (on my bookshelf in the flat I had a book on folksong, *Among the Old Scotch Minstrels*, written by McDowall and signed by him on the flyleaf). Amazingly, then, it is likely, that that manuscript, and perhaps others, graced the drawing room of my drawing room flat.

And so my first meeting with Hamish Henderson led me inevitably to my home, my life and the scholarship and writing that has occupied me since.

There is one special place, of course, where Henderson will never be forgotten. Sandy Bell's, erstwhile known as the Forresthill Bar, has been the centre of the Scottish folk scene in

Edinburgh for some time. It was also Henderson's other 'office' and many days he would wander down from the University in George Square to the pub, although it his latter days, the distance sometimes proved too much for him. The atmosphere is summed up by Ailie Munro:

> What is it that draws people like a magnet to Sandy's, to crowd the single room with its Edwardian decor and its awkward shape, long and narrow? The friendly atmosphere, of course, and the social drinking, but one of the chief attractions over the last years has been the hope of hearing some music, spasmodic though it may be: the exciting possibility that a music session may erupt, like a volcano from the seething, flow of that 'submerged world'. You may be having an engrossing conversation (and these four old walls seem to draw out good talk) with a miner, a tapestry weaver from an old-town studio, a doctor from the nearby Infirmary, a university lecturer escaping from academia, a mother relegating for a while the awesome responsibility of young children, a labourer, an unemployed teacher, a visiting world-famous authority on some subject, or a well-known alcoholic on whom the manager keeps a watchful eye… when suddenly, right beside your ear or at the farthest corner of the room, you hear it. At first only audible in the hubbub: a jig, hornpipe or reel on the fiddle or penny whistle, or from a group of players; a voice raised in an old ballad or a song written last week; a rollicking, ranting tune belted out by a trio of young men; the dancing, irresistible lilt an accordion, or the moan of the older concertina now enjoying popularity. But what happens after those first strains percolate depends

on two things: the quality of the music, both content and performance, and the kind of people who happen to be present, for without the right vibrations nothing worthwhile will happen.[3]

I have known Sandy Bell's ('Bell's'; I was always told that only those who knew the original 'Sandy Bell' could call it 'Sandy's') for many years. It served a key function in the folk revival – not only as a centre for musicians, but also the birthplace of the *Sandy Bell's Broadsheet*, a key source of information for the Scottish folk scene.

Bell's was (is), of course, just a pub, and the scene of just about everything, good or bad, in its time. But it served as an important and democratic focus for the dissemination of Henderson's work. Henderson would meet a range of people there, friends like George Gunn, William Montgomerie, Freddy Anderson, and countless others, or a wide range of visiting scholars singers or artists from all the airts. Many times, nothing much happened, but sometimes you might go there and get inveigled in a session that lasted all day. I remember one time going in for a quick lunchtime pint to find a company that included Henderson, the novelist Alasdair Gray and a bearded gentleman known as 'the King of Scotland'. Just about anything could happen there. Angus Calder recalls a similar experience:

> I remember a day in 1981 when I dropped into Bell's for a half pint before lunch and came out busy seven hours later. Hamish Henderson had presided over an impromptu colloquium involving Tom Leonard, Cathal (McConnell), Andy school teacher Glasgow call Lorna never seen by any

of us before not, by me, since. She had I mostly nodded and smiled while Cathal played, Tom the cited stanza after stanza of 'B V' Thomson from memory, and Henderson reminisced, sang, and reminisced more. There was no kitschy, self-conscious posturing, no beery flirtation – it was all serious pleasure, the communion on some high frontier of Culture to which Henderson had led us…[2]

Sandy Bell's reminds us that Henderson's world was no academic ivory tower, or even anything like that! Henderson took the literary and folk tradition out into the world and knew many people. There are many frequenters of Bell's who remember Henderson, not as a scholar or writer, but as a drinking buddy. The pub serves now as a sort of shrine to him, with pictures, poems and songs framed on the wall.

But, in his latter years, drink and declining health took its toll on Henderson, and, in his last few years his achievements in teaching and writing grew fewer, although he still corresponded with and nurtured friends. Even after his death, however, Henderson's spirit still seemed to remain in Bell's. One strange thing happened in Bell's on the day of Henderson's funeral (many of us had decamped there). I was standing at the bar with Raymond Ross when I saw someone come in. 'That looks like Eddie Linden', I said, 'I thought he was dead!' 'So did I,' said Ray (a newspaper had actually, accidentally, published his obituary). Eddie had 'come back to life' for Henderson's farewell; He would have appreciated the irony!

Some of the things that Henderson fought for have not come to pass. That does not mean that he was a failure; it means that they are still worth fighting for. And they are, but perhaps in a way that is reconstituted for the new technological, political and socio-economic world of today.

He drew scholars and enthusiasts from everywhere to the School of Scottish Studies. Sadly, that is now largely a graduate school and Scotland has no centre for the folk tradition to rival Cecil Sharp House in London or The Irish Traditional Music Archive in Dublin.

Henderson inspired me, so much of my own work draws from his creative spiirit. Another person he inspired and supported was Carlos Arredondo, the Chilean historian, poet and songwriter who came to Scotland after the Pinochet coup. Carlos notes:

> [Hamish Henderson was] a person who always supported my work and took part in Solidarity events for Chile... [Hamish] was once in my home for dinner conversing and singing old Italian Partisan songs to my Italian mother-in-law who was visiting us in Edinburgh. Hamish had been during the war a British intelligence officer in Italy. My mother-in-law was surprised to see Hamish singing songs that she had learned during the war and was thrilled with the experience. Henderson loved Antonio Gramsci. He had been one of the first to translate his work from Italian into English. Hamish, the poet, the song collector, and composer of *The Freedom Come-All-Ye* was a socialist and a true internationalist. We shared a platform several times. In 1986 I asked him if he could help me to find a record company to record my songs and he did. Only in 1989, however, I could record my songs. I asked him if he could write a few words about my record *Debo Cantar Bonito* and he ended up writing three pages full

of beautiful things.[4]

Carlos Arredondo and Ian Spring, from contrasting backgrounds and interests, but two of the hundreds of singers, scholars, artists, etc who were inspired and supported by Henderson.

For my part, I have tried to identify as honestly as possible, the areas in which Hamish Henderson succeeded and failed in his career. He was a superb collector of folksong, an innovative poet who, in the end didn't quite produce the major work that the latter part of his life deserved. He managed, in writing very few songs, to produce well-loved masterpieces. He wrote with passion about folksong but didn't produce, as many hoped, the major work on Scottish folksong that we still await. He was also the first to translate Antonio Gramsci's *Prison Notebooks* and translated the work of other notable European poets.

Personally, I believe that Henderson was a much more complex individual than his public persona ever revealed. Dick Gaughan comments on this:

> Perhaps the only real way to remember and understand Hamish is to embrace the apparent contradictions – poet and polemicist, Internationalist and Nationalist, warrior and pacifist, realist and romantic, traditionalist and modernist, brashness masking shyness, intellectual confidence hiding personal insecurities. I knew Hamish the legend and I knew Hamish the human being. And, for all the times we drank, fought, argued, debated, sang and laughed together, I think! probably knew the former better.[5]

Finally, what is the answer to the question I raised in the first part of this essay: did Henderson achieve the results in creative output and scholarship that his talent promised? There is only one answer. If you count also the poems, songs, essays, etc that came from those he nurtured, supported and championed, his achievement is immense.

References:

1. Ian Spring, *Phantom Village: the myth of the new Glasgow* (Edinburgh: Polygon, 1990).

2. From a piece was written by Dick Gaughan for the *Herald* newspaper following Henderson's death in 2002).

3. Ailie Munro, *The Folk Music Revival in Scotland* (London: Kahn and Averil, 1984), pp 18-19. Strangely, Ailie Munro was not a common frequenter of the pub. See also Gillian Ferguson, *The Story of Sandy Bell's: Edinburgh's World Famous Folk Bar* (Beauchamp: Matador, 2014).

4. From a note provided by Carlos Arredondo.

5. From a piece was written by Dick Gaughan for the *Herald* newspaper following Henderson's death in 2002).

APPENDIX ONE: HAMISH HENDERSON: AULD REEKIE

1. Floret Silva Undique

Floret silva undique,
The lily, the rose, the rose I lay.

Tell-tale leaves on the elm-tree bole;
Reekie's oot for a Sabbath stroll.
Tim and Eck from their pad in Sciennes—
Cowboy T-shirts and Brutus jeans;
Gobstopper Gib and Jakie Tar,
Billies oot the Victoria Bar,
And Davie Bowie plyin' his trade
The sweetest minstrel was ever laid.

Foret silva undique,
The rocker, the ring and the gowans gay.

The bonniest pair ye iver seen
Play chasie on the Meedies green.
Undressed to the nines, frae tit tae toe,
The Kimmers o' Coogate are a' on show.
Ripper o' flies, lord o' the tools,
Yon mental boot boy Eros rules.

Floret silva undique
The rockin' righteous are makin' hay.

Oot from their dens, as shair's your life,
Come Knox the poxy and Mac the Knife
Major Weir o' the twa-faced faith,
And Deacon Brodie in gude braid claith.

Floret silva undique
We'll hae a ball, though the Deil's to pay.

The quick and the slaw are game for a tear;
Sma 'back snooves from his Greyfriars lair.
Out of the darkmans the queer coves come,
Janus guisers from bield and tomb:
Scrunchit hurdies and raw-bone heid
Junkies mell wi' the livin deid.
Get stuck in Homie, and show's the way.
The lily, the rose, the rose I lay.
Seely sunshine and randy mirk
Like Auld Nick's wing ow'r a pairish Kirk.
Whae's yon chattin' up Jess Mackay?
It's Bailie Burke, wi' his weet wall-eye.
The kinchin's bara, so clinch the deal:
gie her a note, son, and hae a feel.
Edina—Reekie—mon amour.
Dae't, or I'll skelp your airse, ye hoor.
The flesh is bruckle, the fiend is slee:
Susanna's elders are on the spree.
The bailie beareth the belle away.
The lily, the rose, the rose I lay.

Floret silva undique
Sweet on the air till dark of day.

Sma'back pipes and they dance a spring.
Over the grave all creatures sing.
The sun gangs doon under yon hill
Jenny and Jake are at it still.
To the greenwood must I go alas
Could you gie me a loan o' Balaam's ass?
Alano I dig you the most:
The lily I laid, the rose I lost.
Whit dae ye hear amang the broom?
Spreid your thies, lass, and gie me room.
Twa gaed tae the woods, and three cam hame
Reekie, tell me my true love's name.
Edinburgh castle, toun and tour
The gowans gay and the gilliefloor.
Luvers daffin' aneath the slae
Floret silva undique
The bonniest pair ye iver seen
Fuckin' aneath the flooer'in' gean.
Baimies wankin' abuin the clay

Floret silva undique
Flora is queen of lusty May
The lily, the rose, the rose I lay.

2. Auld Reekie's Roses

That hoor the dawn is rouging
The Portobello Road.
A clapper over cobbles
The lorries bum their load.

Lay the lily O
O lay the lily O

Through Jessie's wanton window
A single bulb still bums.
The tall chain-smoking chimney
Stands by while Jessie earns.

At stair and close and vennel
The grimy day keeks in.
The wayside pulpit calls us
To keep it free from sin.

Wake up, wake up Alanna
The room is full of light.
I've got to earn my loving
It can't be always night.

Alonie and alonie
You'll have to bide your lane.
There's Woodbines in the dresser
And a lolly for the wean.

He walks down by the fun-fair
A cold forsaken den.
Tarpaulin drapes the gee-gees
Til Destry rides again.
A breeze from Inchcolm swithers,
Flakes oot amang the groins.
The bells of doom come jangling

From Calvin's stony loins.
Day empty day advances:
A siren skreichs in pain.
Up vennel, close and stairheid
The wifies mak their mane.

O would you be a sodger
And list with Sergeant Death—
Queen's shillings in his sporran
And whisky on his breath.

Or would you be a charmer
Aloft where angels sing?
The monumental mason
Will clip that angel's wing.

Lay the lily O
O lay the lily O

Day empty day advances
Gives lightsome dawn the lie.
The wayside pulpit calls us
To seek our joys on high.

The brothel-banks are open—
They cater for all needs.
The fozy voyeurs gather
To watch how money breeds.

But when the fun-fair opens

And bairnies ride the range,
The Oriental Gambler
Will snitch their smallest change.

Lay the lily O
O lay the lily O

Wake up then Camerados
It's time to make a move.
You can't be aye beach-combing
On lucky shores of love.

The brothel-bank's for busting,
The inmates all set free.
The Kirk, that dour dissembler,
We'll brak its back in three.
This seely Earth's our Salem
To Hell with Kingdom Come.
If Sergeant Death struts near us,
We'll slash his painted drum.

The wayside pulpit's dredgy
Can soond for ither lugs.
The joys o' Heaven we'll leave til
The angels - and the speugs.

Lay the lily O
O lay the lily O
Lay the lily O
O lay the lily O

3. The Flyting o' Life and Daith

Quo life, the warld is mine.
The floo'ers and trees, they're a' my ain.
I am the day, and the sunshine
Quo life, the warld is mine.

Quo daith, the warld is mine.
Your lugs are deef, your een are blin
Your floo'ers maun dwine in my bitter win'
Quo daith, the warld is mine.

Quo life, the warld is mine.
I hae saft win's, an' healin' rain,
Aipples I hae, an' breid an' wine
Quo life, the warld is mine.

Quo daith, the warld is mine.
Whit sterts in dreid, gangs do on in pain
Bairns wintin' breid are makin' mane
Quo daith, the warld is mine.

Quo life, the warld is mine.
Your deidly wark, I ken it fine
There's maet on earth for ilka wean
Quo life, the warld is mine.

Quo daith, the warld is mine.
Your silly sheaves crine in my fire
My worm keeks in your barn and byre

Quo daith, the warld is mine.

Quo life, the warld is mine.
Dule on your een! Ae galliard hert
Can ban tae hell your blackest airt
Quo life, the warld is mine.

Quo daith, the warld is mine.
Your rantin' hert, in duddies braw,
He winna lowp my preeson wa'
Quo daith, the warld is mine.

Quo life, the warld is mine.
Though ye bigg preesons o' marble stane
Hert's luve ye cannae preeson in
Quo life: the warld is mine.

Quo daith, the warld is mine.
I hae dug a grave
I hae dug it deep,
For war an' the pest will gar ye sleep.
Quo daith, the warld is mine.

Quo life, the warld is mine.
An open grave is a furrow syne.
Ye'll no keep my seed frae fa'in in.
Quo life the warld is mine.

APPENDIX TWO
HAMISH HENDERSON: THREE SONGS

1. The 51st Highland Division's Farewell to Sicily

The pipie is dozie, the pipie is fey,
He winna come roon' for his vino the day.
The sky ow'r Messina is unco an' grey,
An' a' the bricht chaulmers are eerie.

Then fare weel ye banks o' Sicily,
Fare ye wee I ye valley and shaw.
There's nae Jock will mourn the kyles o' ye,
Puir bliddy swaddies are wearie.

Fare weel, ye banks o' Sicily,
Fare ye weel, ye valley and shaw.
There's nae hame can smoor the wiles o' ye,
Puir bliddy swaddies are wearie.

Then do on the stair and line the waterside,
Wait your tum, the ferry's awa'.
Then doon the stair and line the waterside,
A' the bricht chaulmers are eerie.

The drummie is polisht, the drummie is braw
He cannae be seen for his webbin' ava.
He's beezed himsel' up for a photy an a'
Tae leave wi' his Lola, his dearie.

Sae fare weel, ye dives o' Sicily
(Fare ye weel, ye shieling an' ha'),
We'll a' mind shebeens and bothies
Whaur kind signorinas were cheerie.

Fare weel, ye banks o' Sicily
(Fare ye weel, ye shieling an' ha');
We'll a' mind shebeens and bothies
Whaur Jock made a date wi' his dearie.

Then tune the pipes and drub the tenor drum
(Leave your kit this side o' gthe wa').
Then tune the pipes and drub the tenor drum
A' the bricht chaulmers are eerie.

2. The John MacLean March

Hey, Mac, did ye see him as ye cam' doon by Gorgie,
Awa ower the Lammerlaw or north o' the Tay?
Km man is comin' and the haill toon is tumin' oot:
We're a' shair he'll win back to Glasgie the day.
The jiners and hauders-on are marchin' frae Clydebank;
Come on noo and hear him, he'll be ower thrang tae bide.
Turn oot, Jock and Jimmie: leave your crans and your muckle
gantries,
Great John MacLean's comin' back tae the Clyde!
Great John MacLean s comin 'back tae the Clyde!

Argyle Street and London Road's the route that we're
marchin—

The lads frae the Broomielaw are here—tae a man!
Hi, Neil, whaur's your hadarums, ye big Hielan teuchter?
Get your pipes, mate, an' march at the heid o' the clan.
Hullo Pat Malone, sure I knew ye'd be here son:
The red and the green, lad, we'll wear side by side.
Gorbals is his the day, and Glasgie belongs tae him:
Ay, great John MacLean's comin' hame tae the Clyde.
Great John MacLean s comin' hame rae the Clyde!

Forward tae Glasgie Green we'll march in good order:
Wull grips his banner weel (that boy isna blate).
Ay there, man, that's Johnnie noo—that's him there, the bonnie fechter,
Lenin's his fiere, lad, an' Liebknecht's his mate.

Tak' tent when he's speakin', for they'll mind what he said here
In Glasgie, oor city—and the haill warld beside.
Och hey, lad, the scarlet's bonnie: here's tae ye, Hielan' Shony
Oor John MacLean has come home tae the Clyde!
Oor John MacLean has come home tae the Clyde!

Aweel, noo it's feenished I'm awa back tae Springburn,
(Come hame tae your tea, John, we'll sune hae ye fed).
It's hard work the speakin'. Och, I'm shair he'll be tired the nicht,
I'll sleep on the flair, Mac, and gie John the bed.
The haill citie's quiet noo: it kens that he's restin'
At hame wi' his Glasgie freens, their fame and their pride!
The red will be worn, my lads, an' Scotland will march again

Noo great John MacLean has come hame tae the Clyde,
Noo great John MacLean has come hame tae the Clyde.

Hey, Mac, did ye see him as ye cam' doon by Gorgie,
Awa ower the Lammerlaw or north o' the Tay?
Km man is comin' and the haill toon is tumin' oot:
We're a' shair he'll win back to Glasgie the day.
The jiners and hauders-on are marchin' frae Clydebank;
Come on noo and hear him, he'll be ower thrang tae bide.
Turn oot, Jock and Jimmie: leave your crans and your muckle
gantries,
Great John MacLean's comin' back tae the Clyde!
Great John MacLean s comin 'back tae the Clyde!

3. The Freedom Come-All-Ye

Roch the wind in the clear day's dawin
Blaws the cloods heelster-gowdie ow'r the bay,
But there's mair nor a roch wind blawin
Through the great glen o' the warld the day.
It's a thocht that will gar oor rottans
—A' they rogues that gang gallus, fresh and gay—
Tak the road, and seek ither loanins
For their ill ploys, tae sport and play

Nae mair will the bonnie callants
Mairch tae war when oor braggarts crousely craw,
Nor wee weans frae pit-heid and clachan
Mourn the ships sailin' doon the Broomielaw.
Broken faimlies in lands we've herriet,

Will curse Scotland the Brave nae mair, nae mair;
Black and white, ane til ither mairriet,
Mak the vile barracks 0' their maisters bare.

So come all ye at hame wi' Freedom,
Never heed whit the hoodies croak for doom.
In your hoose a' the bairns o' Adam
Can find breid, barley-bree and painted room.
When MacLean meets wi's freens in Springburn
A' the roses and geans will turn tae bloom,
And a black boy frae yont Nyanga
Dings the fell gallows o' the burghers doon.

REQUIEM
(for Hamish)

Oh, what blethers there were in Sandy Bell's,
And the pipers of Princes Street out for a blow,
And high jinks in the Pleasance,
And ashes scattered in the Perthshire snow

St Mary's, thrusts its tripart glory
into the crushing December sky.
Life and death are flyting in the aisle;
the heroic runners of Cyrene boast their last hurrah
then finally lay to rest
with the ghosts of the Sibhe,
(And Eddie Linden risen from the grave)
And once again you, at the centre of things.

In this old kirkyard-laden city,
bones settle into stone
and the barroom clock ticks
until the Lord calls last orders;
the final dram, the ultimate song,
and a pibroch bursts and beckons
to the long walk home.

INDEX

The flooers and trees,
I am the
Quo